COUNTRIES OF THE WORLD

Italy

Gareth Stevens Publishing
MILWAUKEE

About the Author: Josephine Sander Hausam is a former teacher with a master's degree in English literature. She currently works in a small town library in New York's Hudson Valley. Her poetry and feature articles have been published in magazines and newspapers.

PICTURE CREDITS

Giulio Andreini: 3 (bottom), 5, 9 (bottom), 22, 52, 53, 66, 75
Bes Stock: 1, 3 (center), 4, 11 (top), 12, 42
Camera Press Ltd.: 15 (bottom), 29 (top), 62, 63, 69, 80, 81, 82, 83 (all)
Paolo Ciucci: 9 (top), 54, 55
Sylvia Cordaiy Photo Library: 47 (top)
Focus Team Italy: 3 (top), 7, 40, 57, 74, 79
Haga Library Inc., Japan: 2, 8, 20, 21, 24, 26, 28 (left), 29 (bottom), 38, 39, 41, 44, 56, 60 (top), 61, 67, 68, 70, 71, 85, 91
HBL Network Photo Agency: 23, 28 (right), 30 (both), 33, 46, 84
Ingrid Horstman: 27
The Hutchison Library: 19
Illustrated London News Picture Library: 13, 15 (center)
Sheila McKinnon: 10, 89
North Wind Picture Archives: 11 (bottom), 15 (top), 45, 60 (bottom), 76 (both), 77, 78
Chip & Rosa Peterson: 51
Pietro Scozzari: 48, 58, 87
Still Pictures: 73
Topham Picturepoint: 14, 16, 17, 18, 32, 49, 50, 59, 64
Travel Ink: 47 (bottom)
Trip Photographic Library: Cover, 6, 25, 31, 34, 35, 36, 37, 43, 65, 72

Digital Scanning by Superskill Graphics Pte Ltd

Written by
JOSEPHINE SANDER HAUSAM

Edited by
GERALDINE MESENAS

Designed by
JAILANI BASARI

Picture research by
SUSAN JANE MANUEL

First published in North America in 1999 by
Gareth Stevens Publishing
1555 North RiverCenter Drive, Suite 201
Milwaukee, Wisconsin 53212 USA

For a free color catalog describing
Gareth Stevens' list of high-quality books
and multimedia programs, call
1-800-542-2595 (USA) or
1-800-461-9120 (CANADA).
Gareth Stevens Publishing's
Fax: (414) 225-0377.

© **TIMES EDITIONS PTE LTD 1999**
Originated and designed by
Times Books International
an imprint of Times Editions Pte Ltd
Times Centre, 1 New Industrial Road
Singapore 536196
http://www.timesone.com.sg/te

Library of Congress Cataloging-in-Publication Data
Hausam, Josephine Sander.
Italy / by Josephine Sander Hausam.
p.   cm. -- (Countries of the world)
Includes bibliographical references and index.
Summary: Surveys the geography, history, government, language, customs, and culture of Italy.
ISBN 0-8368-2310-9 (lib. bdg.)
1. Italy--Juvenile literature. [1. Italy.] I. Title.
II. Series: Countries of the world (Milwaukee, Wis.)
DG417.H38   1999
945--dc21   98-52428

Printed in Malaysia

1 2 3 4 5 6 7 8 9 03 02 01 00 99

Contents

AN OVERVIEW OF ITALY

A peninsula extending far into the Mediterranean Sea, Italy was at the center of Western civilization for hundreds of years. Today, it is a crossroads of people and professions, where the old and new, the functional and beautiful, are combined in a dynamic, modern country.

This book is about Italy's contrasting features: its prosperity and its poverty; its ornate splendor and its simplicity; its early history of division and its future as a united country; its wet Alpine winters and its dry Mediterranean summers; its artistic treasures that lure millions of visitors and its problems that cause millions of citizens to emigrate. Many contrasts coexist in this picturesque country.

Opposite: **The Santa Maria della Salute stands regally across the Grand Canal in Venice, where gondolas wait for tourists.**

Below: **Many of Italy's artistic treasures have been meticulously restored to halt the damaging effects of time and pollution.**

THE FLAG OF ITALY

The Tricolore — the Italian flag — consists of three panels of green, white, and red. It was first adopted by a few Italian city-states in 1797, when Napoleon Bonaparte had control of the region. The Tricolore was a variation of the flag of the French Revolution. The blue in the French flag was replaced with green, a symbol of nature and, hence, of man's natural right to liberty and equality. In 1848, the Tricolore became the first symbol of national unity, and, in 1861, it became the flag of the Kingdom of Italy and included the coat of arms of the king. In 1946, when Italy became a republic, the royal coat of arms was removed.

Geography

A Land of Mountains

Italy is shaped like a high-heeled boot and is the fourth largest country in Western Europe, after France, Spain, and Germany. The total land area, including the islands of Sicily and Sardinia and other smaller islands, such as the picturesque Isle of Capri, is 116,333 square miles (301,302 square kilometers).

The Italian peninsula has about 5,000 miles (8,045 km) of coastline washed by four seas, each a branch of the larger Mediterranean Sea. In the west are the Ligurian and Tyrrhenian Seas; in the east, the Adriatic Sea; and in the south, the Ionian Sea. Italy is bordered on the north by France, Switzerland, Austria, and Slovenia.

Mountains crisscross Italy. The country's northern region is dominated by the Alps, a 900-mile (1,448-km) long, curving arch of high peaks, including Mont Blanc, which touches the clouds at 15,771 feet (4,807 meters). In the past, the Alps acted as a natural barrier between Italy and central Europe. One low-lying point,

EARTHQUAKES IN ITALY

Italy is prone to many natural disasters, one of which is earthquakes. The regions of Naples, Umbria, Abruzzi, and Friuli-Venezia Giulia are the areas most subject to tremors that have taken lives and destroyed property. (*A Closer Look, page 52*)

Below: The Dolomites lie in northeastern Italy near the Austrian border. These mountains are a favorite destination of skiers during the winter months.

the Brenner Pass, connects Italy and Austria and once served as an important trade route. It was also a route used by conquering armies sweeping into Italy.

Extending down the center of Italy like a backbone are the Apennines, a mountain range where steep slopes and canyons in the north make travel difficult and isolate many small villages.

Italy's largest plain, the Po Valley, is situated in the north, surrounded by mountains. Watered by the Po River, the valley is densely populated and heavily farmed. Many tributaries or small rivers feed the Po as it flows to the Adriatic Sea. Other major rivers include the Arno, which flows through the city of Florence, the Tiber in central Italy, which flows through the capital city of Rome, and the Volturno, in the area near Naples. The rivers in the south do not have a steady flow of water. They might flood during the winter, then dry up during the summer.

Thousands of years ago, glaciers that still exist on high slopes in the Alps gouged out portions of land in northern Italy and created a series of long, narrow lakes. These large lakes include Maggiore, Lugano, Como, and Garda. Other lakes fill the craters of extinct volcanoes.

CITIES FROZEN IN TIME

Some of the mountains in Italy are active volcanoes. In A.D. 79, Mount Vesuvius near Naples erupted and buried the ancient cities of Pompeii and Herculaneum under ash, mud, and rock. Excavations have been carried out on the sites of these ancient cities since 1748. Archaeologists have uncovered columns of temples, courtyards, and everyday items.
(A Closer Look, page 46)

Seasons

Although the word *sunny* is often associated with Italy, and the country is in the temperate zone, which suggests pleasant year-round weather, the climate is actually unstable.

The position of the sea and the mountains affects the weather, causing rapid changes in temperature and rainfall from region to region. The Alpine region has long, cold winters and short, cool summers. The Po Valley has a continental climate, with cold, snowy winters and hot, humid summers. Most rain falls in the spring and autumn, and fog is frequent around the lakes.

VENICE: A SINKING CITY

The city of Venice floods as often as ten times a year. The cause of the flooding is a combination of natural phenomena, including high winds that push the sea toward Venice.

(*A Closer Look, page 72*)

Left: Snowcapped Monte Cervino lies on the border between Italy and Switzerland, in the picturesque region of Valle d'Aosta. Better known as the Matterhorn, Monte Cervino stands at 14,780 feet (4,505 m). It is one of the tallest mountains in Europe.

A cold northeast wind, called the bora, occasionally blows in from the Adriatic region and can reach speeds of up to 100 miles (161 km) per hour.

Down through the Apennines, winters are cold and rain is heavy in all seasons except summer. The western coastline has a maritime climate with frequent rain. Winters are cool, but there is not much variation in temperature during the year. For example, in Rome, average temperatures range from 54° Fahrenheit (12° Centigrade) to 88° F (31° C).

The southern coastal area of Italy is dry, warm, and sunny. Sometimes, hot dry winds, called the sirocco, blow north from Africa into southern Italy, covering the land with a fine layer of reddish sand from the Sahara Desert.

A Scarcity of Plants and Animals

Over its long history, Italy has lost many of its woodlands. Today, only about one-fifth of the country is covered with trees. Natural forests exist in the mountainous regions, which are covered with oak, beech, chestnut, fir, larch, and pine trees. Shrubs, mosses, lichens, and wildflowers grow at high elevations.

In the lowlands of the Po Valley, poplars, willows, alders, and oaks have been planted to replace the original forests, which were cut down to make room for cities and farms. Cypress trees and umbrella pines grow in central Italy.

The gnarled trunks and small, silvery leaves of hardy olive trees cover the hillsides in many regions of Italy. An olive tree must be thirty years old before it bears fruit, but it can continue to produce olives for hundreds of years. Cork, prickly pears, agave, and eucalyptus survive in the dry climate of southern Italy.

Wild boars roam the mountains of Sardinia, but few other wild animals remain in Italy. Most animals and birds have disappeared due to the destruction of habitat and over-hunting. Some animals, such as chamois (small antelopes), black bears, foxes, roe deer, ibex (a kind of goat), and wolves, survive in remote mountain areas. Wood grouse, falcons, and swallows are common birds found in Italy. Sharks, octopi, tuna, swordfish, sponges, sardines, and anchovies live in the Mediterranean Sea.

THE HOWL OF WOLVES RETURNS

In the 1970s, there were only about a hundred wolves left in Italy. Wolf conservation projects, however, are helping to restore the Italian wolf population. Today, there are between 400 and 500 wolves in national parks and nature reserves across the country.
(A Closer Look, page 54)

Left: Italy is one of the world's largest olive oil producing countries. Olive oil is one of its most important agricultural crops. Although olive trees are a common sight in the hilly regions of Italy, the more important olive orchards are those in the southern regions of Calabria and Apulia.

History

Early Tribes

More than six thousand years ago, hunters from northern and eastern Europe crossed the Alps and entered the land that became Italy. Little is known about these first Italians because they left no written records — only pieces of pottery and tools. At some point, these people formed tribal groups and spread to different regions of the peninsula.

The Etruscans

A group of people known as the Etruscans first appeared as a culture in central Italy around 800 B.C. Some scholars believe they came to Italy from an eastern Mediterranean country. Their forerunners came to Italy around 1200 B.C. and established fortified city-states from the Po Valley south along the Tyrrhenian coast to the regions of Latium (including Rome) and Campania. They interacted with native tribes wherever they went and had a strong influence in early Rome. The Etruscans were nature worshipers skilled in art, metal crafts, and sports. Many Etruscan artifacts are preserved in museums.

Below: Some of the earliest settlers in Italy were sea traders from the Middle East called the Phoenicians, who first arrived around 1000 B.C. Three centuries later, in the eighth century B.C., Greeks set up outposts throughout the southern mainland. Temple Valley in Agrigento, on the island of Sicily, has some of the most beautiful Greek temple ruins in Italy.

Left: **This sculpture shows a she-wolf nursing Romulus and Remus, who, in Roman mythology, were the twin sons of a vestal virgin and the god Mars. According to legend, the brothers, abandoned as babies, were found and cared for by the she-wolf until a shepherd discovered them. Romulus has been credited with founding the city of Rome in 753 B.C.**

The Roman Empire

One of the wealthiest areas under Etruscan control was the city of Rome. In 510 B.C., Rome broke from Etruscan rule and established a republic that lasted five centuries. The republic ended when Julius Caesar, a Roman general, became sole ruler in 49 B.C. Caesar expanded Roman rule across much of Europe. He was murdered in 44 B.C. In 29 B.C., his great-nephew, Octavian, was proclaimed the first emperor of Rome and took the name Augustus. For the next two hundred years, a rare time of peace and stability, called the Pax Romana, existed throughout the Empire.

Medieval Italy

Threats from Germanic tribes and economic problems caused the decline of the Roman Empire. In A.D. 476, the Goth leader Odoacre overthrew the last Roman emperor.

Meanwhile, the Christian popes in Rome gained political influence. In A.D. 800, Pope Leo III crowned Charlemagne, a Frankish king who ruled much of Europe, Holy Roman Emperor. For a while, Charlemagne united northern and central Italy. After his death, however, this unity dissolved, and rivalry among princes and popes reigned for three hundred years.

ANCIENT ROME

The ancient Romans enjoyed lavish lives, filled with pleasures and entertainment. Ancient Rome was a very civilized society, and resembled present-day Rome.

(A Closer Look, page 44)

The Renaissance and Foreign Rule

Starting in the eleventh century, independent city-states dominated Italy and contributed to the development of the arts and sciences during the Renaissance. Many countries wanted to control the wealth of Italy, and European nations launched invasions. The French came first, followed by the Spanish. Eventually, Austria ruled northern Italy. From 1796 to 1814, the French returned under Napoleon Bonaparte, who created the Kingdom of Italy, naming himself king. When his rule ended, the victorious monarchies of Europe divided up Italy.

Risorgimento and Unification

In 1833, a period called Risorgimento (ree-sor-gee-MEN-toh), or resurgence, Giuseppe Mazzini led a secret society that worked for national unity and an independent Italian republic. In 1848, revolutions with demands for democratic rights spread through Europe. Austria defeated the revolutions in northern Italy.

Victor Emmanuel II's prime minister, Camillo di Cavour, negotiated with France to help Italy fight the Austrian army. In 1859, Austria finally lost control of northern Italy, which was then ceded to the Kingdom of Sardinia. In 1860, a force of one thousand rebels, led by Giuseppe Garibaldi, captured southern Italy. In March 1861, Victor Emmanuel II declared the conquered lands to be part of the Kingdom of Italy. Ten years later, France withdrew from Rome, and it became the Italian capital.

Below: **The Vittorio Emanuele II Monument in Rome celebrates Italian unification. It is named for Victor Emmanuel II, the king of the independent monarchy of Sardinia-Piedmont, who supported Italian unification.**

The World Wars and Fascism

When World War I broke out in 1914, Italy pledged neutrality but later supported the Allies and declared war on Austria-Hungary. Although Italy was on the winning side, more than 350,000 men were killed, the land was severely damaged, and war debts needed to be paid. Italians were angry with the government.

A loud voice of dissent came from Benito Mussolini, a former journalist and soldier. In 1919, he headed a movement called fascism. The fascists were militaristic, believed in strict government control of labor and industry, and often resorted to violence. In October 1922, Mussolini and 25,000 followers threatened to use violence to seize power in Rome. To avoid an uprising, King Victor Emmanuel III named Mussolini prime minister. By 1925, Mussolini was dictator of Italy under the title of *Il Duce* (il DOO-chay), or "the leader." He ruled until 1943.

In the 1930s, Adolf Hitler, also a dictator, controlled Germany. His invasion of Poland in 1939 led to World War II, and Italy joined forces with Germany. Italian efforts in the war were disastrous, and the country became a battlefield. When American and British troops invaded Italy in July 1943, parliament voted Mussolini out of office and declared war on Germany. In April 1945, Mussolini was executed. The war ended in May.

The Italian Republic

From 1861 to 1946, the Italian flag had three vertical stripes of red, white, and green, with the royal coat of arms in the center. The coat of arms was removed when Italy became a republic.

In 1946, Italian men and women (who had just been granted the right to vote) decided their country should be a republic, not a monarchy. Italy's last king, Umberto II, the son of King Victor Emmanuel III, abdicated after a short thirty-four-day reign.

A new constitution was effected in 1948, restoring the rights of the Italian people and the freedoms the fascists had destroyed. A parliamentary system of government was reinstated.

In 1949, Italy became a member of the North Atlantic Treaty Organization (NATO), a defensive alliance of the United States and European nations against communist aggression. In 1955, Italy was admitted into the United Nations. Italy was also a founding member of the European Economic Community (EEC) — changed to the European Community (EC) in 1993 — a union of European nations concerned with trade and monetary issues.

Today, although many Italians are calling for changes within their country, the Italian government remains one of the most lively democratic systems in the world.

Below: **The 1997 NATO Summit in Madrid, Spain, brought world leaders together, including Italy's former prime minister Romano Prodi** *(back row, fourth from right)* **and United States president Bill Clinton** *(front row, fourth from left).*

Julius Caesar (100−44 B.C.)

During the period of the Roman Republic, Julius Caesar was a brilliant general who conquered England and Germany. He led a large army and enjoyed great popularity. In 49 B.C., he took over the republic and declared himself "Emperor for Life." While in power, he quashed other revolts and attempted to carry out reforms, such as land redistribution and work provisions for the unemployed. His reign was cut short when the aristocrats of the ruling Senate, who objected to his dictatorial rule, killed him on March 15 in 44 B.C., the "ides of March" on the Roman calendar.

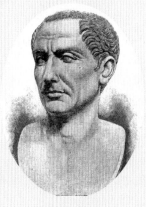

Julius Caesar

Giuseppe Garibaldi (1807–1882)

In 1833, French-born Giuseppe Garibaldi took part in a failed revolt against the king of Sardinia. He then returned to France, and, three years later, left for South America, where he fought for Uruguay against Argentina and became a war hero. In 1848, Garibaldi went back to Italy to help the Lombards fight the Austrians. In 1860, he raised a volunteer force of one thousand red-shirted men and conquered Sicily. In 1862 and 1867, Garibaldi and his red-shirts tried to capture Rome — but failed. Rome did not become part of the kingdom of Italy until 1870. When Garibaldi died in 1882, he was mourned as a national hero in a state funeral.

Giuseppe Garibaldi

Benito Mussolini (1883−1945)

Benito Mussolini was a teacher, soldier, and journalist before he became the leader of the Italian fascists in 1919. In October 1922, King Victor Emmanuel III named Mussolini prime minister when his 25,000 followers, called Blackshirts, marched through Rome and threatened violence. The fascists governed Italy until 1943.

Although Mussolini provided employment through public works projects and financed plans for productive farming, he also took away the citizens' rights to vote and eliminated the country's democratic constitution. His decision to join the Axis powers in World War II destroyed his fascist dictatorship. In 1943, he was arrested, and, in 1945, he was killed by Italian freedom fighters when he tried to escape.

Benito Mussolini

Government and the Economy

Organization of the Republic

Since the end of World War II, there have been over fifty governments in Italy, all of them dominated by the Christian Democrats. The governments have been very short-lived, in power for an average of less than a year each. Italy is the only Western democracy in which one political party has dominated the government.

The Italian government consists of a Parliament with a Chamber of Deputies and a Senate. Representatives of both houses serve five-year terms. A two-thirds majority vote of Parliament elects a president, who serves a term of seven years and is the head of state and commander of the armed forces. The president is responsible for appointing a prime minister, who is the head of government. The prime minister selects cabinet members and establishes government policy.

The prime minister and cabinet members have no fixed terms of office, but Parliament can pass a vote of "no confidence" and

COUNTRIES WITHIN A COUNTRY

Mainland Italy contains two tiny independent states completely surrounded by Italian territory: the Republic of San Marino and Vatican City.
(*A Closer Look, page 50*)

REGIONS

Italy is divided into smaller political units, called regions, similar to the states of the United States or the provinces of Canada. The country is divided into twenty regions. Each region can make its own laws, but the central government has power over all regions.

Left: **Italy's former prime minister Romano Prodi, who headed the center-left coalition, was elected to Parliament in 1996.**

16

force the prime minister and his cabinet to resign. The president also has the power to dissolve the government, at which time new elections would be held.

Above: **Political rallies are boisterous events in election years.**

The Constitutional Court of Italy has fifteen appointed judges. Five of these judges are nominated by the president, five by Parliament, and five by judges of similar rank.

Political Parties

Although one political party has dominated most postwar governments in Italy, there are actually three major parties: the Christian Democrats, the dominant party in Italian government for many years; the Democratic Party of the Left, formerly the Communist Party; and the Socialist Party. At least nine parties contest each election, so most Italians find a party that suits their ideas about government. Over 85 percent of the electorate vote. So many parties create an active political life, however, they also make the country difficult to govern.

THE MAFIA

In the early nineteenth century in Sicily, brotherhoods were formed to protect people from corrupt government officials. These brotherhood organizations soon became so powerful they controlled the highest ranking members of government.

(A Closer Look, page 62)

Striving for Prosperity

Italy is one of Europe's most prosperous countries. Before World War II, the economy was based primarily on agriculture. After the war, many factories were built with aid from the United States. Italy later joined European trade associations, and many products were sold to a growing European market. Tourism is also a vital source of income.

In spite of a high gross national product (GNP) — the value of goods and services produced by a country in a year — Italy faces major problems, such as high social spending; an economy dominated by large, inefficient, government-controlled

Below: **Citrus fruits, such as oranges, lemons, and limes, are important agricultural crops in Italy.**

companies; and in southern Italy, high unemployment. The government has been trying to follow a stricter economic policy, and, at the end of 1997, it announced that the country had met most of its economic goals.

Agriculture and Fishing

Most Italian farms are small and family-owned. Principal crops are sugar beets, tomatoes, grains (such as corn, rice, and Durham wheat for pasta), grapes (for wine), and olives (for olive oil). Italy is the world's second largest producer of olive oil. Orchards of citrus fruit, cherries, and apricots, as well as almonds, are found in southern Italy.

ITALIAN CARS: THE DREAM INDUSTRY

Italian cars are the most coveted in the world. The beauty of the Ferrari and the functionality of the Fiat are unrivaled. The automobile giant, Fiat is also one of Italy's largest corporations and contributes substantially to the country's GNP.

(A Closer Look, page 58)

Italians raise beef and dairy cattle, pigs, goats, chickens, and buffalo. Herds of sheep roam the island of Sardinia, and goats are common in southern Italy and Sicily. Italy also has a plentiful supply of swordfish, tuna, mullet, mussels, shrimp, squid, and octopi in its waters. Freshwater trout are raised in inland lakes.

Natural Resources

Marble has been quarried from the Italian Alps for two thousand years. Renaissance sculptors searched the rock walls for flawless pieces. It is used for everything from floors to table tops. Peaks of solid white encircle the town of Carrara, the marble capital of the

world. A million tons of marble are cut each year, yet there seems to be enough to last for another thousand years. Other minerals with which Italy is well-supplied are mercury and sulfur.

Manufacturing

The cities of Milan, Turin, and Genoa form an industrial triangle in northern Italy. Cars, computers, and chemicals are produced there. The textile industry, which produces silk, cotton, wool, and synthetics, is another chief source of income. Italy is well-known for the style and quality of its clothes. Buyers from around the world go to Milan for fashion shows. Other industries include machine tools, iron and steel, appliances, and processed food.

Above: **Italy's historic and artistic heritage attracts millions of visitors each year, more people than many of the museums and the narrow medieval streets can handle. The population of some cities doubles during the tourist season, and in July and August, the beaches swell with sunseekers. Tourists provide an essential source of income for this country.**

People and Lifestyle

Early Settlers

Italy has attracted many different groups of people over its long history. The earliest inhabitants came from central Europe and southern Russia more than six thousand years ago. Phoenicians established villages on the islands of Sicily and Sardinia in about 1000 B.C. A few centuries later, the Greeks set up outposts in Calabria and Campania. They spread through the southern mainland, bringing with them their advanced social customs and religious beliefs.

The Etruscans developed culture in the Tuscany region in central Italy in about 800 B.C. After the 4th century, Germanic tribes arrived from the north, followed by other foreign invaders, such as Arabs. Normans and Gauls came from what is now France and built farms and cities during the eleventh and twelfth centuries. Later, Spain controlled the south and Austria ruled in the north. This mix of people in Italy has resulted in an interesting and complex ethnic heritage.

A SHRINKING POPULATION?

In 1992, Italy recorded the world's lowest birthrate — less than two children for each couple. Nevertheless, it has one of the largest populations in Europe, with 57.3 million inhabitants. Over the years, millions of Italians have emigrated to other countries. Large Italian populations exist in other European countries, as well as in Argentina, Australia, Brazil, Canada, and the United States.

Left: Many groups of people have settled in Italy over the centuries, resulting in a population descended from all the major cultures of the world.

Left: **The immigrant population in Italy is always increasing. Recently, groups from North Africa, Asia, and the Middle East, as well as war refugees from Yugoslavia and Albania, have settled in Italy. Many of the bigger Italian cities attract gypsy families from Eastern Europe.**

Regional Differences

The Italian word *regionalismo* (REE-gee-oh-nah-LEEZ-moh) means "loyalty to a particular region." Italians have many local traditions and take pride in them.

In the past, regionalism was intensified by the fact that villages had little contact with each other because of Italy's mountainous terrain. Each village developed its own culture within the larger Italian culture. The differences show up in regional food and folk costumes. The separation between villages also gave rise to hundreds of Italian dialects, with variations in words and pronunciation.

The most problematic regional difference in Italy is between the North and the South and is based largely on economics. The North is the center of Italy's prosperous industries and wealth. In contrast, some southern villages have no roads, and uneducated peasants try to farm land that has deteriorated as a result of deforestation over the centuries. Today, the government is trying to transform the South into a productive region.

City and Country

About a third of Italians live in urban areas. Rome is Italy's largest city, with just under three million people. Naples is the most densely populated city, with poor housing and narrow streets. Fewer people live on the mountain slopes of the Alps and the Apennines and in southern Italy. At one time, many farmers moved to the cities in search of work. Today, however, many people are leaving the overcrowded cities to live in the suburbs, where housing is cheaper and there is less traffic.

Everyday Life

Most Italians live in modern apartments or century-old houses. The very poor live in shacks. Wood is scarce in Italy, so most roofs and floors are made of tiles. Walls are made of stone or concrete, which is an invention of the ancient Romans.

Italians generally keep their homes neat and clean. The kitchen is for cooking, while a room known as the *sala da pranzo*

Left: **Italian families crowd the city squares on Sundays.**

Above: **The Venetian floating market presents a unique way to shop for food.**

(SAH-lah dah PRAHN-zoh) is for eating. A formal room, called the *salotto* (sah-LOH-toh) is for watching television, reading, and formal entertaining. Children often share bedrooms. Most Italian homes have balconies that provide extra space for plants and laundry, as well as a post from which to watch neighborhood life.

In northern Italy, the workday lasts from morning until late afternoon. In central and southern Italy, most offices close in the middle of the day for two or three hours. People go home for lunch, then return to work.

Shopping

Shopping for food is often done at small, local markets stocked with fresh fruit, vegetables, and meat. Most cities have supermarkets, but in remote country villages, there is usually a general store that sells almost everything.

Tobacco stores in Italy serve multiple purposes. Each tobacco store has a special government license to sell postage stamps, legal documents, and special stamps for renewing passports and drivers' licenses.

Elegant shops that sell clothes, shoes, leather goods, and gift items can be found on special streets in the middle of most towns. One of these famous shopping streets is the Via Condotti in Rome.

Education

Some Italian schools are privately run, but most are run by the government. The school year starts in September and ends in mid June. The school day runs from 8:30 a.m. to 1:30 p.m., when children go home for lunch. In the afternoon, they do homework or play sports. The most popular sport with Italian boys is soccer. Girls seem to prefer volleyball and basketball.

Unlike their American counterparts, Italian students attend school on Saturdays. They have two weeks of vacation at Christmas, two weeks at Easter, and nearly three months in the summer. Because the summer vacation is so long, most children have to do "vacation homework" to review what they learned during the school year.

The Italian education system has several stages. Some children start school before the age of six at a kindergarten or nursery school. School attendance is compulsory for all Italian children between the ages of six and fourteen.

Children attend primary school for five years, starting at the age of six. At age eleven, they take an examination to gain entry to middle school, or secondary school, for three years. Here, decisions are made about the kind of studies the students will

MARIA MONTESSORI AND THE CHILDREN'S HOUSE

Maria Montessori, an Italian doctor and educator, revolutionized the way children were taught through the creation of the Montessori system. This method focused on the student's potential to learn, with the teacher acting only as a guide.
(A Closer Look, page 64)

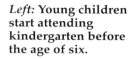

Left: Young children start attending kindergarten before the age of six.

pursue in the future. At the age of fourteen, after passing an examination, a student may leave school. It is likely, however, that he or she will continue studying in a secondary school. Three types of secondary schooling are available. The first is the *liceo* (lee-CHAY-oh), which offers academic courses specializing in languages, the arts, or sciences. The second is a technical institute, which offers vocational courses concerned with commerce, industry, or agriculture. A third choice, the *magistrale* (mah-gee-STRAH-lay), prepares students for a teaching career.

At the end of five years, a student takes a nationwide exam to gain admission into an Italian university. Italy's first university was founded in the city of Bologna in 1135. Today, Italy has fifty-nine universities in thirty-six cities. Over 1.2 million students go to universities, and only three percent of Italians aged fifteen and older are illiterate.

Language, art, cooking, fashion, graphic design, and music are some of the courses foreigners study in Italy.

Left: A Christmas Mass is being celebrated in the church of Santa Croce in Florence.

Religion

Girls in fancy white dresses and boys in neat blue suits walk down the aisle of a Roman Catholic Church to receive their First Communion. This ceremony is a common sight in Italy, where about 95 percent of the population is Catholic.

Vatican City, a separate city-state located within the city of Rome, is the spiritual and governmental center of the Roman Catholic Church. Many hospitals, schools, and charities are run by the Church. Catholicism is the dominant religion in Italy and plays an important role in daily life.

In addition to Catholics, small groups of people belong to Protestant denominations and to the Jewish faith. The number of Muslims in Italy is also growing due to increased immigration from North Africa. In southern Italy, many Catholics also follow folk beliefs, and some women are said to possess magical powers.

SAINTS

Most Catholics are named after a saint, a holy man or woman given special recognition by the Church. Each saint is honored on a specific day of the year. In addition to celebrating birthdays, Italians also celebrate "name days," or the feasts of the patron saints after whom they are named.

Every Italian village and city also has a patron saint who is expected to protect the people. In return, the people worship the saint with prayers and have a festival every year on the saint's feast day.

Honored more highly than all the saints is the Virgin Mary, the mother of Jesus. She is the queen of Italy's spiritual life.

The History of Roman Catholicism

During the Roman Empire, a Roman governor named Pontius Pilate ordered the execution of a political prisoner in A.D. 33. The prisoner's name was Jesus. By the year A.D. 64, followers of Jesus, called Christians, who believed Jesus was the son of God, were living in Rome. In that year, the Roman Emperor Nero accused the Christians of starting a fire that destroyed the city and ordered hundreds of them to be put to death. Many Romans believed that Nero himself started the fire.

Christianity was only accepted in Rome three hundred years later. One morning before a battle, a Roman leader, Constantine I, saw a vision of the Christian cross in the sky. Constantine's troops won the battle, and he legalized Christianity in Rome.

In A.D. 324, Constantine built a church over the tomb of St. Peter, who was an apostle of Jesus. In the fifteenth century, the old church was rebuilt. Over the next two centuries, architects developed a new church on that site, called the Basilica of St. Peter. This sacred shrine is the center of Vatican City, the world capital of the Roman Catholic Church.

Left: **John Paul II was elected pope in 1978, becoming the first Polish pontiff. The pope is considered a spiritual father to all Roman Catholics. He also has absolute rule over Vatican City and is the ultimate authority within the Catholic Church.**

Language and Literature

The Birth of a National Language

In 1870, when King Victor Emmanuel II of the newly united country of Italy arrived in Rome, he said, "Well, we've finally made it!" He spoke, however, in a language that was understood only by the people of the Piedmont region. Until that time, there had been no common national spoken language in Italy. In order to unite the country, a common language was needed. One Italian dialect, based on the language used during the fourteenth and fifteenth centuries in the city of Florence, was chosen as the basis of modern Italian.

The Italian Language

It took another one hundred years before most of the country learned to use "official" Italian. Now it is taught to children in schools and is heard on radio and television.

Italian is a melodious language. Its roots come from Latin, the language of the Roman Empire. Latin survived the fall of the empire and became an international language used in science and philosophy and in the Roman Catholic Church.

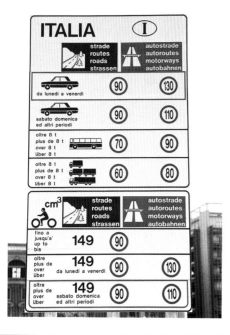

Far left: **Most road signs in Italy are presented in four languages — Italian, French, English, and German.**

Left: **Dante Alighieri was Italy's greatest poet. His Christian epic, *Divina comedia (The Divine Comedy)*, is one of the greatest literary works of all time and the first major work written in the Italian vernacular, rather than in Latin. This epic poem describes the poet's journey through hell, purgatory, and heaven.**

Dialects

The official Italian word for white is *bianco* (bee-AHN-koh). In parts of Piedmont, it is pronounced *biank* (BEE-ahnk). In Liguria, it is *giancu* (jee-ahn-KOO); in Campania, *iango* (ee-ahn-GOH); in southern Calabria, *aspro* (AH-spr-oh); and in eastern Sicily, *iancu* (ee-ahn-KOO). Different words, accents, and pronunciations of a particular region, city, or village is what is known as a dialect.

Many Italian dialects originated from variations of ancient Latin and other Italic languages. Over time, they became so different that people in one region could not understand people in another region. There are still some areas of Italy where the local dialect is the only language spoken. For example, on the island of Sardinia, most people speak Sardo.

Dialects are primarily spoken, not written, and some have disappeared. In the hopes of preserving Italy's past, they are being written down and recorded.

Foreign languages are spoken in some border areas of the country. German is heard near Austria, French in the Piedmont region, Croatian near the city of Trieste, and Greek and Albanian in southern Italy.

Above: **Umberto Eco is a renowned literary critic, semiotician (student of signs and symbols), and novelist. His first novel, *Il Nome della Rosa (The Name of the Rose)*, was an international bestseller. A film version of the book, starring Sean Connery and Christian Slater, was made in 1986.**

Literature

Italy's greatest poet is Dante Alighieri, who wrote *The Divine Comedy* between 1308 and 1321. This epic poem was the first major work written in the everyday speech of Italian, rather than Latin. It is considered one of the most influential works in Italian literature.

Before Dante, classical Latin writers, such as Catullus, Horace, Virgil, Pliny, Livy, Tacitus, Juvenal, and Ovid, wrote vivid stories of ancient Rome. At the time Dante was writing, Giovanni Boccaccio collected 100 short stories in his book, *The Decameron*. Petrarch also developed the poetic sonnet.

In the 1500s, Niccolo Machiavelli wrote his famous book, *The Prince*, which describes ways to be a ruler. Later, Baldassare Castiglione's *The Book of the Courtier* tried to guide people in proper manners at court.

Italy's rich literary tradition continued through the centuries. Luigi Pirandello , a playwright from Sicily, won the Nobel Prize for Literature in 1934. Another writer, Italo Calvino, is famous for his fables.

Below: **A well-known children's story, *Pinocchio*, about a puppet who comes to life, was written by an Italian, Carlo Collodi.**

Arts

Painting and Sculpture

From the statues and terra cotta vases dating back to the days of the Etruscans, art has always been a part of the Italian landscape. In ancient Rome, paintings decorated homes and public buildings, and sculptures based on Greek and Roman mythology adorned squares and palaces. When the Catholic Church became powerful in Italy, art was used to convey religious stories and beliefs.

From the fourteenth through the sixteenth century, Italy was the center of incredible activity in art, when artists rediscovered older ideals of beauty from Greek and Roman classical times and developed new ways of presenting them. This period is known as the Renaissance, which means "rebirth." While much of Renaissance art was produced for the church, it showed the glory and beauty of humanity. Portraits by Botticelli, frescoes by Michelangelo, sculptures by Bernini, and oil paintings by Titian show the rich and detailed spirit of the Renaissance. Museums, such as the Uffizi in Florence; churches; and the Vatican, where the Sistine Chapel is located, display many masterpieces.

In the nineteenth century, Giorgio de Chirico was famous for his dreamlike paintings, and, in the twentieth century, Amedeo Modigliani gained worldwide acclaim for his modern portraits.

Above: **Modern Italian painter Amedeo Modigliani's portraits are world renowned.**

LEONARDO DA VINCI: A GENIUS

Instead of flat figures on a canvas, one of Italy's greatest artists, Leonardo da Vinci, painted scenes, such as *The Last Supper*, in a way that created a sense of perspective and depth. Besides being a talented artist, Leonardo da Vinci was also a brilliant scientist and inventor.

(*A Closer Look, page 60*)

Left: **Raphael was one of the greatest painters and architects of the Italian High Renaissance. His famous fresco, *School of Athens,* can be seen in the Stanza della Segnatura, Pope Julius II's papal apartment in the Vatican.**

Left: **The largest outdoor theater in ancient Rome, the Colosseum, covers six acres (2.4 hectares) and still stands today.**

Architecture

Art in Italy is not just in museums. It is everywhere, especially in the architecture. Arches, columns, windows, doorways, steps, and even fountains reveal a variety of artistic styles.

Theaters; temples, such as the Pantheon; baths; and public buildings from two thousand years ago remain intact throughout Italy and other parts of the former empire. Buildings from the Middle Ages still stand in many hill towns in Italy, along with cathedrals built in Romanesque and Gothic styles. Gothic architecture features pointed arches, stained glass windows, and soaring spaces. One of Italy's greatest cathedrals is the Duomo of Orvieto, which took three hundred years to build.

During the Renaissance, designs based on classic Greek and Roman styles were reintroduced. Carefully proportioned bell towers, massive domes, elegant palaces, courtyards with decorative columns, and cathedrals with rounded, symmetrical designs and curved walls were financed by wealthy citizens and by the church. Florence is especially known for its many architectural wonders from the Renaissance. The best example in Rome is St. Peter's Basilica.

More recent buildings of interest include the Mole Antonelliana in Turin, which, when finished in 1897, was the tallest building in the world, and the Pirelli skyscraper in Milan, an elegant example of modern Italian architecture.

TRADITIONAL CRAFTS

Many unknown Italian artists quietly share their talents by creating traditional crafts. These artisans make ceramics, glass, paper, jewelry, and violins. In Venice, glassblowers have practiced the skill of creating clear, light, elegant glass for a thousand years, and papermakers, like those in the Museum of Paper in Fabriano, still produce paper by hand. Gold, silver, and platinum jewelry are also some of Italy's principal exports. Wood carvings, sculptures in alabaster and marble, rugs, embroidery, lace, hand-wrought ironwork, and straw hats and mats are other handicrafts that provide tourists with souvenirs.

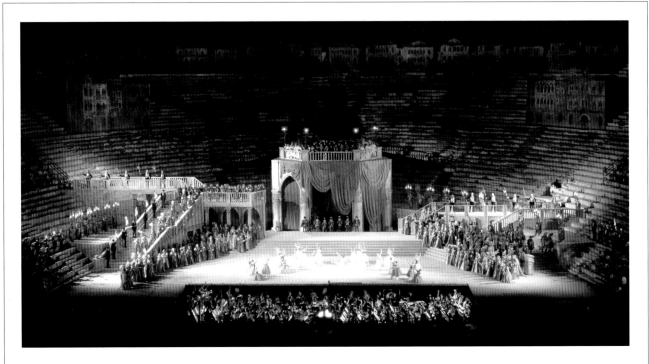

Music

Italian composers, musicians, singers, and musical inventions have given the world beautiful music.

In the sixth century, Gregorian chant was developed in the Catholic Church. In the eleventh century, a monk named Guido d'Arezzo created a system of writing down music. Madrigals (an aristocratic form of poetry and music) appeared during the Renaissance. Opera and orchestral music developed in the 1600s and sonatas (instrumental pieces for one or two instruments) in the 1700s. The violin, cello, and piano all are Italian creations.

The very words used to describe music are, in fact, Italian: *solo* (soh-loh), meaning alone; *largo* (lahr-GOH), meaning slow; *allegro* (ah-LEH-groh), meaning fast; *forte* (FOHR-teh), meaning loud; and *pianissimo* (pee-ah-nee-SEE-moh), meaning very soft.

Italian Opera

Italians are passionate about opera. This musical form tells a story with orchestral music and singers. Many of the world's greatest operas, such as *Aida, The Barber of Seville,* and *Madame Butterfly,* were composed by Italians. Two outstanding Italian operatic composers are Giuseppe Verdi and Giacomo Puccini. Enrico Caruso and Luciano Pavarotti are well-loved Italian opera singers of the twentieth century.

Above: La gioconda (The Joyful Girl) **is being performed at the amphitheater in Verona. This opera was composed by an Italian, Amilcare Ponchielli, in 1876.**

THE SECRET PERFECTION OF THE STRADIVARIUS

Three hundred years ago in Cremona, Antonio Stradivari made the greatest violins, violas, and cellos the world has ever known. These musical instruments have great value today and have become treasured possessions of the world's most famous musicians.
(A Closer Look, page 68)

Cinema

In 1990, Giuseppe Tornatore won an Oscar for his film, *Cinema Paradiso,* which means "Cinema Heaven." In part, it is a movie about the powerful impact of cinema in Italy. In the 1950s and 1960s, the Italian equivalent of Hollywood, called Cinema City, flourished outside Rome. During the same period, Italian director Federico Fellini's films won several Academy Awards, bringing Italian cinema to the attention of the whole world.

Before World War II, the fascist government created a national cinema institute where directors' creativity was limited by what the government wanted. After 1945, filmmakers started producing movies about the real, everyday life of Italians. Famous directors include Roberto Rossellini, Vittorio De Sica, and Luchino Visconti. Italian actresses, such as Sophia Loren, and actors, such as Marcello Mastroianni, appeared in these films.

Left: **Sophia Loren is perhaps the best known Italian actress. She enchanted audiences with her beauty in the 1950s and 1960s in several Italian and Hollywood films. Loren achieved international stardom when she won an Academy Award in 1961 for the Italian film, *La ciociara* (*Two Women*), in which she played the mother of a teenage girl in wartime Italy.**

33

Leisure and Festivals

Social Interaction

In his famous book, *The Italians,* Luigi Barzini describes the Italians as energetic, gay, noisy, animated, and happy people crowding the streets, squares, and marketplaces of Italy. Italians are generally regarded as warm, outgoing people, who hold back few emotions. Outsiders think of Italians as excitable because they tend to have discussions in a lively manner, often using gestures and expressions in addition to words. A shrug of the shoulders, a lifted eyebrow, hands waving wildly — all these gestures say something without a word having ever been spoken. When words are spoken, they are likely to be loud and spirited.

Touch occurs frequently and openly among Italians. Friends are greeted with a hug and a kiss. Men stroll with arms on each other's shoulders. Women hold hands. Italians like social gatherings, often meeting in outdoor cafés, restaurants, and private homes. Italians enjoy each other's company as much as they enjoy the food — a vital part of their social interaction.

In almost every town and village, there is a *piazza* (pe-AHT-zah), or open square, where people meet. In large cities, there are sometimes several piazzas, and some are huge.

Below: **Piazzas, such as Venice's Piazza San Marco (St. Mark's Square), are central meeting places for Italians and are often buzzing with activity. Children go there to play. Housewives go there to shop. Men often sit at the café tables there drinking** *espresso* **(ehs-PREH-soh) or wine, playing cards, discussing business, or reading newspapers.**

Left: **A favorite pastime of Italians is sitting at a café and watching the world go by.**

Another traditional form of leisure activity is the *passeggiata* (pah-seh-jee-AH-tah), or walk. Italians enjoy walking around town, especially on Sundays after their main meal.

Vacations

The month of August is devoted to vacations. Stores and factories close, and Italians head for the mountains or the sea. Resort areas often fill up with people desiring a short, relaxing vacation.

Most Italians prefer to remain in their own country during the holidays, but, in recent years, the number of people traveling abroad has increased. Some Italian families own second homes and retreat to them to escape their normal work routine.

News and Entertainment

Over 90 percent of Italian households have at least one television set. Sporting events, films, quiz shows, cartoons, and soap operas are popular programs. Many American shows are dubbed into Italian. In some regions, foreign television is available, including programs from Switzerland in the northern part of Italy. Many Italians also enjoy going to movies and operas.

About five million newspapers are purchased daily in Italy. Magazines abound, from the women's weekly *Grazia* to the music magazine *Rockstar*. Children enjoy reading comics. Walt Disney characters, Garfield, Charlie Brown, and Asterix are popular.

Sports

Soccer is the most popular professional sport in Italy. Every Sunday, the stadiums are packed with fans. Supporters unable to attend the matches watch them on television. In Italy, soccer is not just a spectator sport; it is also played by amateur athletes all over the country.

Italians of all ages enjoy cycling, skiing, car racing, tennis, golf, volleyball, fencing, horse racing, hunting, hiking, and fishing. Bocce is a less strenuous game that resembles bowling, except it is played on a dirt court, and wooden balls are tossed or rolled to try to hit a larger wooden ball. Bocce is distinctly Italian.

An American sport that has caught on in Italy is basketball. Many of the players are Americans who play under contract for a time in the Italian leagues.

Tour of Italy

Visitors walking or driving on roads in Italy might suddenly be surrounded by cyclists, backs bent, hands gripping the handlebars, legs pumping like well-oiled pistons. Most cyclists

SOCCER: THE NATIONAL PASSION

Soccer is the world's most popular sport, and nowhere is it more evident than in Italy. Every large Italian city has a soccer team that competes in a league.
(*A Closer Look, page 70*)

Left: **Every spring, the Tour of Italy bicycle race attracts the world's best riders, who cross the entire length of Italy in three weeks.**

belong to clubs that ride every week. Just as millions of spectators crowd the soccer stadiums, almost as many line the routes of major bicycle road races, which are both difficult and dangerous. Almost every province has its own race. Every May, the Tour of Italy bicycle race, considered the World Series of cycling, attracts the best riders in the world. They cross the entire length of Italy, from Sicily to Milan, in three weeks. Sometimes plummeting down mountain roads, they reach speeds of 60 miles (97 km) an hour. The best professional cyclists earn millions of dollars.

Above: **The Italians' love of racing carries over to cars. One of the most demanding auto races in the world, the Mille Miglia, covers 1,000 miles (1,609 km) of Italy's public highways. A famous race track in Monza in northern Italy regularly attracts avid race fans.**

Snow, Sand, and Sea

Skiing is popular on the slopes of the Alps and the Apennines. In some places, it is possible to ski even during the summer. Italian skier Alberto Tomba has, in his ten-year career, won forty-eight World Cup medals, three gold and two silver Olympic medals, and four World Championship medals.

Water sports, such as sailing, motorboat racing, swimming, fishing, skin diving, and waterskiing, are natural in a country surrounded by water.

Left: **The six-week period before Easter is the time for carnivals throughout Italy. The Viareggio Carnival shown in the picture is one of the most elaborate in the country, with processions of giant floats. Another famous celebration is the Venice Carnival. For ten days, people wear costumes and celebrate in the streets. There is also a procession of gondolas along Venice's Grand Canal.**

Festivals and Holidays

The Italian flair for drama and fun is clearly shown in the great number of festivals held each year throughout the country.

Some festivals have an historical or cultural focus. In July, the Venetians celebrate the end of the plague of 1576 by building a bridge of boats across a canal to the Church of the Redemption.

Verona, the setting for Shakespeare's *Romeo and Juliet,* holds a Shakespeare Festival, and Venice hosts an international film festival every year. The Festival of Unity has a political purpose; held in Grado, Italy, it features debates, concerts, art shows, dancing, and food.

Many festivals honor food. In the wine-producing areas, people celebrate the end of the grape harvest with fairs and dances. Castel San Pietro has a Fair of Mutton Chops, and Torre Annunziata celebrates a Festival of Spaghetti! Festivals are also held to recognize miracles. In Naples, the whole city turns out to see the dried blood (kept in two glass vials) of the local patron saint, San Gennaro, liquefy.

Christmas

Many festivals have religious significance in Italy. One of the most important religious festivals is Christmas. Nativity scenes are set up in churches throughout the country, and children go from church to church to see the beautiful cribs on display. At midnight on Christmas Eve, a mass is celebrated in all the churches. As with all Italian festivals, feasts, holidays, and carnivals, traditional foods are an important part of Christmas. The menus vary from region to region.

THE PALIO

Many Italian festivals are based on ancient regional rivalries. Although horse racing is a sport in Italy, one particular horse race is more of a festival than a contest. It takes place in Siena and is called the Palio.

(*A Closer Look, page 66*)

Left: Holy Week is the most important celebration in Italy. On Easter Sunday, processions are held throughout Italy with marching bands and people in colorful costumes. All Italian Christians are in high spirits as they celebrate the resurrection of Christ.

Food

Food from Other Lands

Pizza, parmesan, pasta, *prosciutto* (proh-SHOO-toh), *cannoli* (kah-NOH-lee), *gelato* (jeh-LAH-toh), *cappuccino* (kah-pooh-CHEE-noh), and wine! Italians love food. It has been said that eating is their favorite activity.

Situated at the crossroads of the Mediterranean Sea, Italy has borrowed food and recipes from many places. For example, marzipan (made from almonds, egg whites, and sugar) came from the Arabs, the use of lemon juice came from the Far East, and tomatoes came from Mexico. By the sixteenth century, cooking had become an art in Italy, and the best of a long tradition survives today.

Regional Specialties

Each region in Italy has its own specialties. Naples is considered the birthplace of pizza. Bologna is famous for *tortellini* (tohr-teh-LEE-nee), a stuffed pasta; Parma is known for its ham, Lombardy for its rice dishes, Tuscany for its soups, Sicily for its sweets, and the Alpine valleys for their cheeses. Some of Italy's famous cheeses are parmesan, gorgonzola, and mozzarella.

Left: Pasta has been a basic Italian staple for hundreds of years. Stone carvings on an Etruscan tomb from the sixth century B.C. show a rolling pin and board for rolling out dough and the small, wheeled instrument used to cut it. Most pasta names describe their shapes. For example, *agnolotti* (AHG-noh-loh-tee) means little fat lambs, *bucatini* (boo-CAH-tee-nee) means little holes, *cannelloni* (kah-neh-LOH-nee) means big pipes, and *vermicelli* (vehr-mee-CHEH-lee) means little worms. Even babies eat tiny pasta shapes called *pastina* (pahs-TEE-nah). The most famous form of pasta is spaghetti. One pasta manufacturer's catalog lists eighty-seven varieties of pasta!

Meal Patterns

Italians have light breakfasts. A sweet roll or bread, along with a cup of milk for children and coffee for adults, starts the day.

The main meal is served midday or in the evening. It usually begins with a plate of appetizers, or *antipasti* (ahn-tee-PAHS-tee), which might include salami, cheese, bread, and olive oil. Next comes soup, usually a beef broth or a thick vegetable soup, such as *minestrone* (mee-neh-STROH-nay). Then comes a plate of pasta. Common pasta sauces are made from tomatoes, others from butter and cheese, and one, called *pesto* (PEH-stoh), is a mixture of olive oil, basil, garlic, and pine nuts. In northern Italy, rice dishes, called *risotto* (ree-SOH-toh) are served in place of pasta, followed by a meat or vegetable dish, and then a salad. The meal ends with fresh fruit.

Desserts are eaten on Sundays and special occasions. They include pastries such as cannoli, cakes such as *zuppa inglese* (ZUH-pah een-gleh-ZEE), marzipan (colored almond paste), and gelato (ice cream). Fresh bread, wine, and mineral water are always on the table. The shape of the bread, which can be sticks, round loaves, or small rolls, varies from region to region. Each region also has its favorite wine. One famous Italian wine is *Chianti* (kee-AHN-tee), a red wine from the Tuscany region.

ICED TREATS: AN ANCIENT SPECIALITY

Gelato is Italian ice cream, which is made differently from American ice cream and contains less fat. Some favorite gelato flavors are coffee, chocolate, rum and raisin, and vanilla.

(*A Closer Look*, page 56)

41

A CLOSER LOOK AT ITALY

Italy has survived centuries of war and devastation caused not only by invading countries but also by natural elements. In A.D. 79, disaster struck the cities of Pompeii and Herculaneum when Mount Vesuvius erupted, burying the two cities under ash, mud, and rock. More recently, small towns in the province of Umbria were destroyed when earthquakes leveled houses.

Below: **Venice's Grand Canal is its main "street," running 2.5 miles (4 km) through the center of the city.**

Beautiful, romantic Venice, has not been spared either. Experts work around the clock to prevent this ancient city from sinking.

In this section, you will discover some of the interesting people, places, facts, and events that are part of Italy. You will learn about the great artist, scientist, and inventor, Leonardo da Vinci; the brilliant doctor who revolutionized childhood education, Maria Montessori; the cultural, religious, and recreational lives of the ancient Romans; as well as how one of the world's most sinister organizations, the Mafia, was started. This section delves into all things Italian, including Ferraris, ice cream, music, fashion, and soccer.

Opposite: **The Vatican security force is called the Swiss Guards, known more for its resplendent uniforms, designed in the fourteenth century by Michelangelo, than for its position as protector of the Pope.**

Ancient Rome

Patches of the original basalt paving stones laid down by the Romans centuries ago still exist on the road called the Appian Way. Its construction began in 312 B.C. to connect Rome to its colonies on the Adriatic Sea. More highways followed, linking Italy to Spain, Turkey, and Syria. Rome became the center of power in the Western world, prompting the expression, "All roads lead to Rome."

In many ways, Rome today resembles the city during the days of the Roman Empire. It was the largest city in Italy, the capital and center of government, a learning center, a religious mecca, a trade and transportation hub, an entertainment hot spot, and a lure for people from all over the world.

The Ancient Romans

The people of the Roman Empire were clearly divided between the free Roman citizens, who had many privileges, and the slave population. Roman women, however, had limited rights and were expected to keep house and raise children. Slave children were expected to work by the age of six or seven. They did, however, find time for fun. Pictures show them playing with hoops, rolling walnuts like marbles, and riding piggyback.

Below: Ancient Rome's influence reached far and wide. Hadrian's Wall in Northumberland, England, is one of the largest Roman ruins in Britain. The Roman emperor Hadrian ordered its construction as a defensive barrier to guard the northern frontier.

The ancient Romans worshiped many gods. Jupiter, the king of the gods, was the most important. There were hundreds of local gods and goddesses. According to legend, Romulus and Remus, the founders of Rome, were the sons of the war god, Mars, and were cared for by a she-wolf.

For leisure, the ancient Romans went to the Circus Maximus, an amphitheater, to watch chariot racing and gladiator fights. They socialized in bathhouses, elaborate buildings with pools in which to wash and relax, an exercise yard, and rooms where board games could be played.

Above: **In oval arenas called amphitheaters, Roman spectators enjoyed the bloodshed of the fights between wild beasts and gladiators, who were slaves or convicts condemned to fight.**

All Roads Lead to Rome

The Romans built wonderful roads, with three levels of substructure beneath the pavement, and even a special grooved pavement in steep areas to keep horses and people from slipping.

The Romans did many things exceptionally well, and, as a result, modern civilization still sees and feels their influence. Besides roads, Roman language, law, and architecture spread throughout the Empire, and they still influence the world today.

Cities Frozen in Time

Lines and scratches on a plaster-walled house show that, in the ancient Roman city of Pompeii, children used to play a game very much like today's tic-tac-toe. The markings on these walls are only a small part of the remnants of a once-bustling city of about 20,000 people.

Living in the Shadow of the Volcano

On August 29, A.D. 79, a young Roman, Pliny the Younger, looked across the bay of Naples and saw a cloud billowing from the top of Mount Vesuvius, an old volcano. Years later, in letters written to the historian Tacitus, he described what he saw. Steam and hot ashes spewed from the crater, followed by flames and streaks of lightning. Ash and pumice stone rained down on Pompeii, and sulfurous vapors choked the inhabitants as they fled toward the sea. The eruptions continued for three days. When they ended, Pompeii and the neighboring town of Herculaneum lay buried beneath 15 to 25 feet (4.6 to 7.6 m) of mud, cinders, and rock.

Nearly sixteen hundred years later, in 1713, a farmer digging a well in the village of Resina (now called Ercolano) found some pieces of marble. These pieces were the first clues that a city was

Left: **Many of the volcanoes in Italy, such as Mount Etna on the island of Sicily, are still active and continue to threaten the cities built beneath them.**

Left: **Archaeologists from all over the world helped in the task of unearthing the town of Pompeii. Today, visitors can walk among its long-buried columns and marvel at the magnificence of this ancient city.**

buried there. Finally, in 1748, intensive excavation and digging uncovered more statues and the ruins of a theater. Resina had actually been built over the site of Herculaneum. Ten years later, excavation began in the area of Pompeii. The work continues.

Where Time Stands Still

You can now walk the streets of Pompeii and get an idea of the city as it was on that fateful day. You can enter the villas of wealthy merchants, see the marketplace, and look up at the columns of temples.

In Herculaneum, buried under a sea of mud, many buildings survived with their roofs intact, preserving everyday household items and utensils. Cooking pots, jars of wine, a carbonized loaf of bread, metalworkers' tools, statues, vases, gladiators' helmets, wall frescoes, coins, and marble floors all tell us about the everyday lives of the ancient Romans.

Preserved in the hardened ash were shells (molds) of the bodies of citizens who lost their lives. By carefully pouring plaster into the shells, archaeologists made detailed copies of the individuals, on which even facial expressions of agony can be seen. A museum in Naples holds some of these remains.

Below: **These bakery grindstones found among the ruins of Pompeii provide a clue as to how the residents might have lived.**

Classy and Flashy Fashion

Italians have an expression, *bella figura* (BEH-lah fee-GOO-rah), which means "nice figure" and suggests style, making the best of oneself, and making a good impression on others. Italy is the perfect place for fashion designers to display the Italian traditions of craftsmanship, good taste, modern technology, and creativity. From the Vatican Guards' Renaissance uniforms to the silvery silk skirt worn by a catwalk model at the Milan Fashion Show to the white leather Gucci handbag, Italians have a flair for elegance, and it sells. The fashion trade is one of Italy's largest industries, together with tourism and the automotive industry. Much of its appeal comes from the designers' skill with fabrics.

The Allure of Silk

Five thousand years ago in China, the art of making silk was such a jealously guarded secret that anyone caught telling outsiders about it was beheaded. Nevertheless, the secret did get out. Silk was produced in Italy in the twelfth century. In the fertile fields of Lombardy in northern Italy, mulberry trees were planted as food for silkworms. Today, silk is also imported from the Far East and Latin America. It is woven into clothes, scarves, shawls, and ties in factories near Lake Como.

Wool and Leather Products

Italy is considered the foremost knitwear manufacturer in Europe. Workers weave, dye, card, design, and knit wool in all its forms and mix it with other fibers. The Italian knitwear company, Benetton, well-known in America, began as a family business in 1965, mass-producing knitwear popular for its bright colors.

Since the Middle Ages, leather has been used by Italy's craftsmen to create objects of rare excellence. In the past, leather was used for horses' harnesses and scabbards for swords; today, it is used for shoes, bags, belts, coats, luggage, briefcases, desk accessories — even hats. Most Italian firms now use sophisticated machinery to make their products, but some leather artisans still practice the age-old tradition of crafting by hand.

Above: **The Italian fashion industry is one of the largest industries in the country.**

Opposite: **When you wear something that says "Made in Italy," you can be certain that it comes from an industry with high standards. Italian fashion designers have become the leaders in their industry. The most famous example is the late Gianni Versace, one of the world's most talented designers, known for his flamboyant and outrageous creations.**

SYNTHETIC FABRICS

Designers in the ready-to-wear world of fashion are turning more to synthetics because of their flexibility. Italian companies produce most of Italy's cotton fabrics for shirtmakers. Cotton is mixed with synthetic fabrics such as polyester and nylon, resulting in a wide range of fabrics.

Countries within a Country

The Republic of San Marino

San Marino is the last surviving city-state from the Italian Renaissance period. Its earliest laws date back to 1253. San Marino was recognized as an independent country by Napoleon in 1797 and by the Congress of Vienna in 1815, but its history goes back much farther, to the fourth century, when a group of Christians fled into the Apennines to escape religious persecution by the Romans.

    With a total area of less than 24 square miles (62 square km), San Marino has a population of more than twenty thousand. The language is Italian (the local dialect is Romagnolo), the country's

Below: **Selling postage stamps to collectors throughout the world is one of the main economic activities of the Republic of San Marino, an ancient independent country located within Italy.**

currency is the Italian lira, and the religion is Roman Catholicism. San Marino has its own government, but this tiny nation's economy depends on the big country that surrounds it.

Vatican City

Surrounded by the capital city of Rome, Vatican City is smaller than the Republic of San Marino. It is only about 100 acres (40.5 ha) and has a population of about one thousand.

In 1929, the Italian government recognized the right of the Holy See (the ruling body of the Roman Catholic Church, which consists of the Pope and the Sacred College of Cardinals) to govern Vatican City.

Two of the largest buildings in the world are in Vatican City — St. Peter's Basilica and the Vatican Palace next to it. Priceless masterpieces of art are found in the church and the Vatican Museum. In front of St. Peter's is a vast piazza, or open square, where thousands of people from all over the world gather to hear the pope speak and to receive his blessing.

Above: **Vatican City has its own bank, railroad station, flag, television channel, postal system, daily newspaper, and radio station (a gift from Guglielmo Marconi, the Italian who invented radio). This city-state also has a police force called the Swiss Guards. St. Peter's Square, however, shown in the picture above, comes under the authority of the Italian police.**

Earthquakes in Italy

On September 26, 1997, a massive earthquake struck the province of Umbria in central Italy, and the entire medieval city of Nocera Umbra, with 6,500 residents, had to be evacuated. The tremors were felt 90 miles (145 km) away in Rome.

Earthly Tremors

The province of Umbria, a mountainous region in the heart of Italy, is known for its small historic towns and old churches. In mere seconds, these ancient churches collapsed, and the valuable artwork in them was damaged. Eleven people died, and thousands had to evacuate their homes.

The first jolt dug deep cracks into the ancient frescoes of the thirteenth-century Basilica of San Francesco in the town of Assisi. Nine hours later, while friars and engineers gathered to examine the damage, a second jolt sent huge sections of the ceiling crashing to the ground. Four in the group were killed. Tremors continued to shake the earth for days.

Left: **In 1997, earthquakes in the province of Umbria destroyed many buildings and left thousands of people homeless.**

Living with Earthquakes

A lot of geological activity occurs throughout the Apennines, the range of mountains running from northern to southern Italy. The country sits on Europe's most active seismic belt. Deep below Earth's surface, the foundations of the mountains are moving slowly to the northeast; earthquakes are the result. According to the National Institute of Geophysics, Italy's seventy-two seismographic centers have registered more than eighty-five hundred earthquakes in recent decades.

The Friuli-Venezia Giulia region in northeastern Italy was severely damaged in 1976. Another serious earthquake occurred in 1980 in the southern part of Italy. Thousands of people died in the villages around Naples. In 1984, many historic towns in Umbria and Abruzzi were badly hit.

Like Californians, Japanese, and other people living in areas with seismic activity, Italians must get used to living with earthquakes.

Above: **The Basilica of San Francesco in the town of Assisi was damaged in the 1997 earthquake.**

The Howl of Wolves Returns

In the early 1970s, there were only about a hundred wolves in Italy. Now, the wolf is on the rebound, with numbers close to five hundred. Wolf range has been expanding northward, and there are wolves in national parks, on farms, and in the suburbs.

In 1976, wolves received official protection in Italy. Some regions offer incentives for shepherds to adopt wolf-defense measures, such as providing special guard dogs.

Wolves kill sheep (over thirty-six hundred near Siena in 1994) because their natural, preferred prey, such as deer, have disappeared with the vanishing forests. To increase the wolf population, Italians have been restoring the natural habitat of these animals. Government agencies and conservation groups have reintroduced deer, chamois, and ibex to the forests. New national parks and nature reserves have also been established, the Parco Nazionale delle Foreste Casentinesi in Tuscany, for example, and the Parco Nazionale d'Abruzzo.

People are just now beginning to realize that animals such as wolves have an important role in the conservation of the natural world, helping to keep the delicate balance between animals and their environment.

Left: **The wolf is a very difficult animal to study. It is shy and avoids contact with humans. It usually lives in wooded areas as part of a small pack, is most active at night, and travels great distances throughout its vast territory. Observing wolves in the wild is certainly a very rare and lucky event!**

Radiotracking

As early as the 1960s, researchers adopted radiotracking as a tool to help them gather knowledge on the habits and ecology of the wolf. In Italy, radiotracking was introduced in the 1970s by Luigi Boitani, who studied wolves in Abruzzi.

With radiotracking, it is possible to follow an animal from a distance and determine its location. This method makes it possible to obtain information on daily movements and migrations; daily, seasonal, and yearly rhythms of activity; home range; habitat use; and even survivorship, size, and structure of entire populations. A device called a radio collar is placed around the wolf's neck, and its signals can be received with antennas operated manually from a vehicle or even from a plane.

When capturing a wolf, it is important not to harm it. The captured wolf is anesthetized, weighed, measured, provided with a radio collar, and released as quickly as possible in the same place it was caught. The batteries of the radio collar will transmit a regular signal for three to four years.

Results of radiotracking studies help wolf researchers better understand and appreciate this fascinating animal. Their studies are also critical to developing effective conservation strategies.

WHY DO WOLVES HOWL?

Wolves howl for many reasons — when they are happy, to keep in touch, when seeking a mate, before they go hunting, and to tell others "Keep out of my territory!" In Rome, a bronze statue of the wolf-mother who nursed Romulus and Remus, the legendary founders of Rome, reminds us of the ancient place of the wolf in Italian history. The long, echoing howls heard today are a good sign that wolves will remain a part of the Italian landscape for a long time to come.

Iced Treats: An Ancient Specialty

Imagine a world without ice cream! In the United States alone, the annual production amounts to about fifteen quarts a year per person. But where did ice cream come from?

A Brief History of Ice Cream

Products resembling ice cream have been traced back as far as the fourth century B.C. In the Middle East, snow and goat's milk were mixed. Around 335 B.C., chilled combinations of fruit juices, milk, and honey were consumed in the court of Alexander the Great of Macedonia (now part of Greece), and it is known that the Roman Emperor Nero ordered a special corps of attendants to bring snow from the mountain peaks for his frozen desserts. With the fall of the Roman Empire, however, this dessert seemed to disappear.

Left: **Like many children the world over, Italian children cannot seem to make up their minds about which wonderful ice cream flavor to choose from the colorful display in the *gelateria* (jeh-lah-teh-REE-ah), or ice cream shop.**

The Italian History of Ice Cream

In the thirteenth century, the Italian traveler Marco Polo returned from Asia with a Chinese recipe combining ice, milk, and fruit. Bernardo Buotalenti from Tuscany then created his own recipe, which, at the time, was a big secret. Because of the high cost of storing winter ice in underground vaults for summer use, only the very rich were privileged enough to indulge in the iced treats.

In 1533, when Catherine de Medici of Venice married King Henry II of France, she served fruit ices at the French court to demonstrate Italy's refined culinary art. She also served a thick, sweetened, semifrozen dessert, more like today's ice cream.

From Italy to the World

In the seventeenth century, a Sicilian, Francesco Procopio de Coltelli, opened the first ice cream parlor in Paris, called "Le Procope." It still stands today. The dessert finally came to the United States with the English colonists.

Today, Italy's typical ice cream, gelato, is made differently from American ice cream, which comes from a standardized mix: half cream, half milk, sugar, and egg yolk, with fruit and nuts added later. Gelato is made in individualized batches created around the flavor. It contains one-third less fat, using 70 percent milk and 30 percent cream.

Italian Cars:
The Dream Industry

The Embodiment of the Italian Dream

It is bright red, has a curved, elegant shape, and holds the road without a sway. It roars with what has been called the spine-chilling howl of twelve cylinders, and costs about U.S. $200,000. It is the ultimate Italian dream. It is a Ferrari.

In 1947, a former race car driver named Enzo Ferrari put a heavy car engine into a light body, stamped the symbol of a prancing horse on the hood, and entered his car in Italian races. By 1949, Ferraris won at least thirty races, including six Grand Prix titles (international races, usually on a risky course).

That same year, Ferrari decided to make cars for the road as well as for the racetrack. He made cars one at a time, using a team of artisans to craft the cars by hand. They became the cars of the rich and famous, and Enzo Ferrari became a legend. When he died at the age of ninety in 1988, his cars had won about five

Below: **The elegance and beauty of the Ferrari has made it one of the most coveted cars in the world.**

thousand races and more than twenty-five world championships. He once said, "A Ferrari should be longed for and dreamed for." The new Ferrari F50 is the latest and most exclusive; only 394 will be built.

Fabbrica Italiana Automobili Torino

While the Ferrari is a dream car, the Fiat, an inexpensive, ordinary, everyday car, created the dream industry of Italy's economy. In 1899, a group of industrialists led by Giovanni Agnelli, a former cavalry officer, created Fabbrica Italiana Automobili Torino — FIAT. Starting in 1914, Fiat produced more than three thousand cars a year. By the mid-1980s, almost one and a half million cars came off the assembly line each year. Based in the city of Turin, Fiat is Italy's largest private employer and is still controlled by the Agnelli family.

The Fiat Punto, introduced in 1993 with the slogan "A car designed by customers to meet their needs," sold two million cars in forty-two months. In early 1997, it was the bestselling car in Europe.

Other well-known Italian cars are the Alfa Romeo, Maserati, Lamborghini, and Lancia, which are luxury cars exported around the world.

Above: **At the Fiat factories, it takes just twenty-two hours to transform a sheet of steel into a finished car, each of which can be tailored to individual demand. Each day, 1,400 models come off the Fiat production line.**

Leonardo da Vinci: A Genius

As a boy wandering the hillsides near the village of Vinci, Leonardo would gaze at birds soaring in the sky and marvel at their flight. As a man in the city of Florence, he visited bird sellers, paid for a caged bird, then opened the cage and let the bird fly away. He studied the beat of the wings. He believed humans could fly if they had the proper wings. He sketched a design for a flying machine, with cloth stretched over wood, to be attached to a man's shoulders, with stirrups for the man's feet to set the wings in motion. Later he changed the design to one with a set of wings attached to a post — a sort of helicopter. He also designed a glider, which could be lifted from the ground by the force of air. To protect fliers from crashes, he invented a "tent roof," or

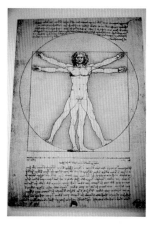

Above: **Leonardo da Vinci was a brilliant scientist. He made amazingly detailed and accurate drawings of human anatomy and plants.**

Left: **In the words of Alessandro Vezzosi, director of the Leonardo da Vinci Museum, Leonardo da Vinci "was a superhuman genius who still has a lot to teach us today."**

parachute. He wrote: "The great bird will make its first flight — filling the whole world with amazement…" Five hundred years ago, his dream failed, but today, Leonardo da Vinci's ingenious inventions have become a reality.

The Universal Man

Born in 1452 in a tiny Tuscan village, Leonardo later worked in the cities for rich noblemen, monks, the pope, and the king of France. With his philosophy of life, "Learning makes the soul young," Leonardo studied, sketched, designed, and painted until he died in 1519 at the age of sixty-seven.

Leonardo's intense creativity and passion for discovery made him a symbol of the Renaissance. He has been called the "universal man." He was an inventor and research scientist, studying anatomy, designing life jackets, underwater goggles and a snorkel, war machinery, a self-turning spit for roasting meat, cork bridges to allow people to walk on water, a minting machine, and a jack for raising churches off the ground. He was also a musician, writer, and, above all, one of the greatest artists of all time.

Leonardo left behind only a dozen completed paintings, but nearly seven thousand drawings. One of his best-known pictures is the Mona Lisa. Generations of people have been bewitched by her half-smile, which seems to suggest secret, soulful thoughts.

The Mafia

Family loyalty, a sense of honor, and respect in the community are seemingly good qualities at the roots of what became, and still is, a sinister, criminal organization known as the Mafia.

The Mafia as a Family Organization

Mafia, a word known in speech but not in writing before 1860, began in Sicily. In one way, Sicily was a region like America's Wild West, where there was not much effective legal law enforcement, and each man had to be ready to defend himself. If violence was needed, it was used, and the man who used it was respected. In Sicily, unlike the legend of the range-riding cowboys, the men lived in one place and had strong family ties. They avenged any slight to the honor of their family. The local "man of respect" became the man of power.

Each boss or family dominated a region. Bosses fought each other. Different criminal groups, with different names, exist in other regions of Italy. One of the better known is the Camorra in Naples. Today, people tend to call all organized crime groups "The Mafia."

Left: **In 1995, Giulio Andreotti, seven-time prime minister of Italy, went on trial for his links with known Mafia organizations.**

Left: The Italian government's battle against the Mafia continues as it seeks to rid the country of corruption and organized crime.

The Mafia Code of Silence

Part of the Mafia story is that the powerful boss actually tried to help ease the harsh life of the peasants by setting the price of crops, giving them access to water, and establishing wages. In return, he demanded not only respect but "protection" money and a code of silence from the Sicilians in his region. Those who informed the police about his criminal activities were murdered.

The *mafiosi* (mah-fee-OH-zee), or members of organized crime, use their power to finance and control certain businesses, such as gambling. Today, their most profitable industry is trade in illegal drugs. It has made the crime families more violent, and the kidnapping of rich people has become a common occurrence.

Dealing with the Problem

The Italian government has been fighting back. Certain judges and lawyers now specialize in Mafia-related affairs. New laws make it easier to convict criminals. Special police units train to deal with organized crime. Today, many young Italians are also determined to free their regions of this serious problem.

Maria Montessori and the Children's House

Maria Montessori wanted low, lightweight tables in different shapes, small chairs, and sofas. Next on her list was a long, low cabinet filled with colored cubes, fabrics, bells, cards with sandpaper letters and numbers, and other materials to see, hear, and feel. She also wanted a chest with little drawers, each containing a card with a name on it, and low-level blackboards. Washstands and a cupboard for each child completed this special room that Maria Montessori called "The Children's House."

This list of items might seem to describe an everyday nursery school classroom, but before 1907 — before Maria Montessori — it was not common at all.

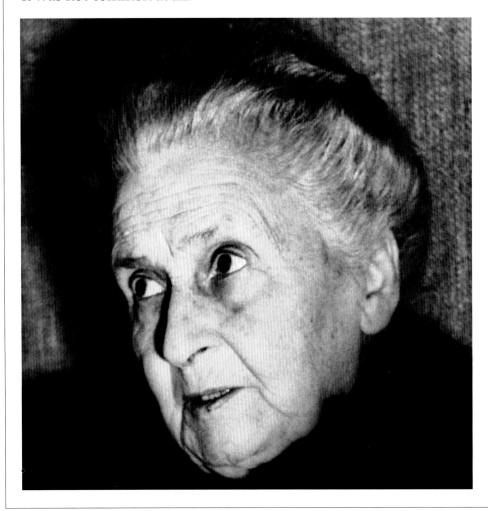

Left: **Maria Montessori left Italy and traveled to England, France, Germany, Holland, Ireland, Spain, the United States, Latin America, India, Sri Lanka, and Pakistan, speaking on behalf of children's rights. She lectured, trained teachers, and wrote many books until her death in 1952.**

The Making of a Brilliant Woman

Born in 1870, Montessori was a bright, bold child. Her parents suggested that she become a teacher, practically the only career open to women at that time. She refused to consider it. Through fierce determination, she became the first female medical student in Italy. After getting degrees in both medicine and literature, she devoted her life to the study of childhood development. She later became a teacher and developed a new theory of education that came to be known as the Montessori Method.

"The Children's House" was the first step. It gave children a place to understand and discover the world around them. The Montessori Method begins with the natural curiosity of the student. A teacher acts as a guide. Maria believed that actions were the key to learning. The teacher or another student first models an action, such as washing dishes, watering a plant, or dancing. The child then practices the same action until he or she masters it. Subjects are taught using real-life objects.

Maria Montessori's method of instruction is now employed in schools around the world. She believed that children have an ability to learn at an early age. As long as an environment is properly prepared, creative materials are used, and directions are clear, the children can teach themselves.

The Palio

Every year, on July 2 and August 16, thousands of spectators jam Siena's main square, Piazza del Campo, to watch the Palio, a bareback horse race. The Palio is a festival that was first recorded in 1283, but it might have had its origins in Roman military training. During the celebration, horsemen, in armor, and footmen parade in rich, colorful costumes from medieval days. To add to the festive atmosphere, flag-twirlers fling brilliant banners high in the air in a colorful performance. This festival has become so popular it is now shown on television in the United States.

The word *palio* (PAH-lee-oh) means "banner." The winner of the race is awarded a silk palio bearing a picture of Siena's patron saint, Saint Catherine. In a procession held before the race, this prize banner is carried around the piazza on a wagon drawn by four white oxen.

Below: Flag bearers dressed in the traditional colors of their *contrada* (cone-TRAH-dah), or neighborhood group, put on a spectacular performance before the start of the race.

A Fight to the Finish

The ancient, walled city of Siena in the Tuscany region is divided into seventeen districts. Each district forms a contrada, with each contrada member wearing the colors of his or her group. Each contrada enters a horse in one of the two races. The contradas choose a horse by lottery, and these horses are blessed at the local churches. Before the race, the horses are displayed in a grand procession. Children often run footraces of their own in anticipation of the real race that is to come.

Once the horse race begins, the rivalry between competitors is great. Riders use whips, not only to spur their horses, but also to lash the other riders. There is little sportsmanship in this race.

The horses go around the track three times, with the race lasting only about 90 seconds. It is a fight to the finish. The winning horse is the one that crosses the finish line first, even if the rider has been thrown off earlier.

The fun does not end after the race. Festivities can last for days. All residents of Siena and visitors to the city join in the festivities as participants and spectators.

Above: **The Palio horse race has no rules, so riders can do whatever it takes to win the race — even bribery is allowed.**

The Secret Perfection of the Stradivarius

Hanging above tiled rooftops like curious laundry, newly varnished violins, which will sell for about U.S. $10,000 each, dry in the sun in the ancient town of Cremona. In shops tucked away on the town's narrow, medieval streets, craftsmen carefully construct violins, trying to reproduce the elusive quality of the Stradivarius violins produced there three hundred years ago — the greatest violins the world has ever known. Today, these ancient instruments of near perfection are auctioned for between U.S. $500,000 and U.S. $1.5 million each.

Antonio Stradivari

Antonio Stradivari (1644–1737), who used the Latin form of his name, Stradivarius, on his instruments, was one of the leading instrument makers in music history. In Cremona, he studied with Nicolo Amati, the grandson of Andrea Amati, who made the first

Below: **Stradivari's extraordinary career spanned seven decades from about 1665, when he was 21, to 1737, when he died at the age of 93. He was an industrious worker, sometimes completing two violins or one cello a month. In 1715, the Polish king ordered twelve violins from Stradivari. Incredibly, the king received all twelve instruments in three months.**

violins in the 1530s. In his lifetime, Stradivari made more than eleven hundred instruments. Today, about 635 violins, 17 violas, and 60 cellos made by him still exist.

The Making of a Stradivarius

Each Stradivarius violin is made from between seventy and eighty pieces of wood of at least seven different types. One type is maple, which is used for the hard back and neck. Spruce is used for the soft front. The wood is aged for up to ten years. Then comes the tedious task of cutting and gluing, after which the wood must be cured for another year before applying about thirty layers of varnish.

Above: **Anne Sophie Mutter, one of today's most talented musicians, is among the few outstanding violinists who perform on a Stradivarius.**

Stradivari would walk the forests of the Dolomite Mountains in search of the perfect wood for his instruments. With great precision and care, he hand-cut beautiful curves (there are no straight lines in a violin), shaved the wood, and joined the pieces with glue to create an almost perfect combination of strength and sweetness of sound — "a sculpture that sings."

The Power of the Stradivarius

Yehudi Menuhin, one of the world's most famous violinists, owns two Stradivarius violins. One was made when Stradivari was ninety years old. The other was made in Stradivari's "Golden Period," when he was seventy-one. According to Menuhin, this violin has "enormous power, great brilliance, a purity and clarity of sound, and a nobility of texture."

One of Stradivari's contemporaries was Giuseppe Guarneri, a master craftsman who worked in Cremona. Giovanni Grancino of Milan also produced instruments suited to the sounds of intimate chamber music.

The Legacy of the Stradivarius

After Stradivari, violins were changed somewhat and were given longer, tilted necks and finger boards, stronger bass bars, and higher bridges. Newer instruments had the volume needed to perform in large concert halls with large orchestras, but the secret perfection of the Stradivari violins has never been reproduced.

Some of Stradivari's instruments are kept in Cremona's city hall. Every morning, one or two are played to keep alive the incredible tones built into them so long ago.

Soccer: The National Passion

In Italy, soccer, known as "football," begins in childhood neighborhood play and culminates in adult professional championships. It is the most popular sport in the country.

The Italian League

The Italian league's first division consists of eighteen teams. Most of the large cities have their own teams. Rome, Milan, and Turin each have two. Players imported from other countries are among the highest-paid employees in Italy.

Below: In the 1930s, Mussolini encouraged the building of stadiums and the creation of regional teams. He believed that a good national soccer team would help promote national pride.

Italians are passionate about soccer, and regional loyalties generate lots of excitement. During the major soccer season, from September through May, noisy fans pack the stadiums on Sunday afternoons to watch the confrontation between teams. Sometimes the enthusiasm of the spectators even causes riots. On Mondays, after the matches, local newspapers devote half their pages to exciting moments in the game.

Italy and the World Cup

In 1930, FIFA (Federation Internationale de Football Associations) organized the first international soccer tournament. The winning team received a trophy called the World Cup. Today, this tournament is held once every four years. Italy won the World Cup in 1934, 1938, and 1982 and was runner-up in 1994. Italy also hosted the tournament twice, in 1934 and 1990.

In the 1990 tournament, Italy played a semifinal match against Argentina. The game was tied at the end of regulation time, requiring two fifteen-minute overtime periods. The two teams were still tied after the overtime, making a shoot-out, with players taking turns shooting for the goal against the goalkeeper, necessary. Argentina outscored Italy and went on to the finals but was defeated by the Federal Republic of Germany.

Soccer Then and Now

Soccer is a universal sport played by more people than any other game. Games involving kicking, throwing, or punching balls toward a goal have existed for centuries. The ancient Romans used to play *harpastum* (HAHR-pah-stoom), in which two teams tried to push a ball over lines drawn behind each opponent. Soccer became an organized sport only in the nineteenth century.

Above: **During soccer matches, the stadiums become a sea of color as** *tifosi* **(tee-FOH-see), or fans, wave banners and flags bearing the colors of their teams.**

71

Venice: A Sinking City

Venice is built on water. Instead of streets, there is a maze of canals flowing around the 118 small islands that make up this city. Gondolas, *vaporettos* (vah-poh-RET-tohs), or motorized boats, and other vessels transport people through Venice and beyond.

Today, the islands are sinking, and the ancient palaces and churches built on them are sinking, too. This sinking is the result of subsoil (the lower layers of sand and clay) in the older parts of the city compacting and settling down. To add to the problem, between October and April, high tides pour through the three entrances into the Venetian Lagoon, flooding the sinking city. The water recedes, leaving silt and mud behind, so the waterways must be dredged and deepened to let boats get through.

ALL CREATURES GREAT AND SMALL

Venice is home to an extraordinary variety of animal and plant life. Green crabs and water rats, pigeons and egrets, algae and sea lavender, all thrive in this rich ecosystem. For five centuries, the city's residents have been working to balance their technological and industrial needs with the needs of nature.

Left: **Gondolas gliding down canals paint a wonderful picture of Venice, hailed as one of the most romantic cities in the world. But this wonderful picture disguises the pollution and flooding problems that have plagued the city for centuries.**

High Tides in Venice

The floods in Venice are caused by a combination of many natural elements occurring at the same time. Venice is located at the junction of the Adriatic Sea and what was once the Po river delta. The Adriatic Sea is susceptible to tidal variations and extremes in atmospheric pressure, which generate high winds. Winds from the north push the sea toward Venice, while winds from the south prevent the tides from flowing back out of the lagoon.

The worst flooding was in November 1966, when St. Mark's Square, the city's lowest point, was under more than 4 feet (1.2 m) of water. By examining the trend of flooding in the past, scientists predict that the next catastrophic flood will occur in 2030.

During floods, rainwater runoff from the square flows into drains that empty into Venice's "main street," the Grand Canal, which extends 2.5 miles (4 km) through the center of the city. When the water rises in the canal, the process is reversed. Water backs up in the drains and flows into the square.

Since the 1966 flood, researchers have been trying to find ways to prevent flooding and protect the ecosystem in the lagoon. A flood warning system has been developed. A system of mechanically operated sea locks is also being developed to control the rising and falling tides at the lagoon's three entrances. This system, however, is a massive engineering project that will take many years to complete.

Above: **During the 1920s, tides about three feet high occurred about once a year. Now, Venice floods up to ten times each year.**

RELATIONS WITH NORTH AMERICA

The United States is one of Italy's most important trading partners. Political relations between the two nations are very stable, although they were not always so amiable. The countries fought on different sides in World War II — Italy with the Axis powers and the United States with the Allies. After the war, the United States helped Italy overcome the ravages of war, and both countries have been on friendly terms ever since.

Left: **The United States' "King of Pop," Michael Jackson, becomes larger than life in Viareggio's Carnival float parade.**

Over the centuries, a continuous exchange of ideas and traditions between Italians and North Americans has enriched both lands. The United States has one of the biggest Italian communities outside of Italy. Italians began emigrating to the United States in the late nineteenth century, to escape the poverty, starvation, exploitation, and drought that plagued their country. By 1910, more than six million Italians had made their home in the United States. Today, just as Italian-Americans have assimilated into American culture, Italian culture, too, has become an integral part of American life.

Opposite: **The island of Sicily is a picturesque tourist spot today. In the mid-nineteenth century, however, it was a chaotic place where organized crime ruled, resulting in the emigration of many Sicilians to the United States and other countries.**

Early Explorers

Some of the most important explorers in history were Italian. In 1492, Christopher Columbus, an Italian from Genoa, sailing under the Spanish flag, reached the islands of the West Indies. He, like other explorers of the time, was looking for a direct trade route to China and India.

After reports of Columbus' voyages reached England, the English king hired another Italian from Genoa, Giovanni Caboto, today known as John Cabot, to sail across the ocean. In 1497 and 1498, Cabot explored the northern Atlantic coastline and claimed it for England. Then, in 1524, the French king hired another Italian, Giovanni da Verrazano, to chart the coast of North America. Today, a bridge named after Verrazano crosses the entrance to New York Harbor.

The name *America,* in fact, was derived from that of an Italian explorer, Amerigo Vespucci, who was born in Florence. Vespucci crossed the Atlantic Ocean and traveled down the coastline of what he thought to be a large continent. He recorded his discovery, and a mapmaker of the time used his name for the newly discovered American continent.

Above: **Amerigo Vespucci was an explorer-navigator who played an important role in the discovery of the New World.**

Early Missionaries and Settlers

In the sixteenth and seventeenth centuries, the Catholic Church in Italy sent missionaries to the New World. They worked among the Native Americans, served as guides for other explorers, and established mission churches in northern Mexico and Arizona.

Italian settlements gradually developed. A small group of Italian glassmakers were part of the Jamestown Colony as early as 1607. Later, in 1657, two hundred Protestant Italians founded New Castle, Delaware. Another colony was founded by Philip Mazzei in Virginia, where he cultivated grapes and olives.

Other Italians also contributed to the development of the new land. During the American Revolution, in the eighteenth century, Giuseppe Vigo, a wealthy fur trader, helped the American colonists in their struggle against British rule. Dramatist and poet, Lorenzo Da Ponte, came to New York in 1805 and became the first professor of Italian literature at Columbia University.

Although the seafaring Italians were the first to land on the shores of America, Italians did not play a major part in America's settlement until the nineteenth and twentieth centuries.

Above: **Italian colonists settled in Jamestown as early as 1607.**

Opposite: **Christopher Columbus, or Cristoforo Colombo in Italian, was born in Genoa in 1451 and went to sea at the age of fourteen.**

Mass Immigration: Who Came and Why?

At the beginning of the twentieth century, Italy was overwhelmed with problems. Poverty and drought brought starvation, and the southern Italian peasants were exploited by rich landowners. In addition, a series of natural disasters struck the land. A disease nearly wiped out the vineyards, Mount Vesuvius and Mount Etna erupted in 1906 and 1910, a series of earthquakes hit in 1905, and an earthquake and tidal wave destroyed most of the city of Messina, Sicily, in 1908. Many Italians fled to the United States to escape appalling living conditions.

Between 1876 and 1930, over five million Italians, mostly from southern Italy, emigrated to the United States. Others chose to go to Brazil and Argentina or to Australia.

The steerage quarters, the cheapest accommodations for passengers on the ships that crossed the Atlantic Ocean, were crowded and filthy. For up to twenty days, Italian immigrants slept in narrow bunks, had no showers, and ate from dinner pails. All discomfort was forgotten, however, when the ships sailed into New York Harbor, and the Italians got their first glimpse of the Statue of Liberty, a symbol of hope and freedom.

Italian immigrants had to pass through the federal immigration facility at Ellis Island, located in the harbor, where they underwent legal and medical processing.

Left: **This picture shows an Italian colony in Mulberry Bend, New York City, in the 1890s. Many Italians migrated to America at the end of the nineteenth century and the beginning of the twentieth century to escape miserable living conditions in Italy. With their poor understanding of the English language and of American ways, however, Italian immigrants had difficulty finding jobs, and many lived in poverty.**

Italian Immigrants: How Did They Live?

Before the late nineteenth century, the majority of Italian immigrants came from northern, industrial regions. The influx at the turn of the century, however, brought large numbers of Italians from the agricultural south. Some of these farmers found work in the fields of New England, the Great Lakes region, and Florida. Others started vineyards in California or worked in the fishing industries on the Pacific coast, especially in San Francisco. Some, usually single men, wandered from town to town, working on the railroads, constructing buildings, or paving roads. Often they sent their pay back to Italy. Sometimes, discouraged, they returned home. Those with families worked in the cities, digging subways, unloading freight, or delivering ice. As they learned English, they became mechanics, bakers, butchers, barbers, and fruit vendors.

Many immigrants worked in their apartments, where their children helped them sew clothes, roll cigars, or make artificial flowers. Sometimes extra workers were hired, and the apartment became a factory called a "sweatshop" because of the long hours and low pay. Most Italian families were poor and often crammed into one or two rooms in run-down, low-rent apartment buildings, with several families sharing a toilet in the hallway.

La Cosa Nostra and Prohibition

Some Sicilians who emigrated to the United States discovered that the ways their people followed in the old country were useful in the new one. They call their organization La Cosa Nostra, which means "our own affair." Americans refer to them as the Mob or the Mafia.

From 1920 to 1933, alcoholic beverages were banned from manufacture and sale in the United States. This period, known as Prohibition, saw the increasing power of the Mafia, which operated bootlegging, or illicit liquor, businesses. Prohibition helped the Mafia rise from disorganized gangs to a powerful, sophisticated organization. Since then, violence between competing gangs has become a part of American life. Well-known crime bosses included Al Capone, Lucky Luciano, and Dutch Schultz. Movies, such as *The Godfather* trilogy and *Goodfellas*, have dramatized the lifestyle of these gangsters.

Organized Crime

After Prohibition ended, organized crime focused on gambling, loan sharking (charging very high fees for loans), and infiltrating and influencing legitimate businesses, such as construction, trucking, and garment manufacturing.

Organized crime is strong in major cities such as New York, Chicago, Los Angeles, Kansas City, Detroit, and Cleveland. The largest concentration of Mafia families is in the New York City area and in New Jersey.

The Government versus the Mob

The U.S. government has been fighting the Mob. Since 1985, the U.S. Justice Department and the Federal Bureau of Investigation (FBI) have prosecuted and convicted the bosses and under-bosses of five crime families — the Gambino, Genovese, Lucchese, Bonnano, and Colombo families — which has led to a decline in their influence. New laws in the United States have also made it easier to convict criminals, and special police units have been formed to deal with this specific problem.

Unfortunately, organized crime continues to appear in new and different forms. It has also become more international, as drugs and money are transported across borders without detection. Law enforcement officials continue the battle.

AL CAPONE

Al Capone, nicknamed "Scarface," was once the most famous gangster in the United States. He dominated organized crime in Chicago from 1925 to 1931.

The son of Italian immigrants from Naples, Capone quit school after the sixth grade and started his criminal career a short time later, when he joined the Five Points Gang. From then on, Capone quickly rose in the ranks of organized crime, ruthlessly assassinating rival gangs. He became the head of Chicago's organized crime in 1925, when he was just twenty-six years old. By 1927, Capone's wealth was estimated to be close to U.S. $100,000,000.

Capone was finally arrested for income tax evasion in 1931 and was sentenced to eleven years in prison. He died in 1947.

U.S. Involvement in World War II in Italy

In 1941, Italy, with the other Axis powers, Germany and Japan, declared war on the United States and the Soviet Union. In 1943, the Allies — the United States and its partners — invaded Salerno, Italy. At this point, the new Italian government, which had replaced Mussolini, began fighting against Germany.

In January 1944, Allied troops landed on the beaches of Italy near Anzio and Nettuno, where some of the fiercest battles occurred. The U.S. Fifth Army lost 107,144 soldiers between January 15 and June 4, 1944. Finally, defeated by the combined efforts of American, British, French, and Polish troops, the Germans retreated, and the Allied forces entered Rome. It was the first enemy capital to be captured, and the Allied victory lowered the morale of the Germans. The following September, the Allies reached Florence, and, in the spring of 1945, they crossed the Apennines and invaded northern Italy.

In April 1945, the war was over, but the destruction and poverty remained. Allied troops stayed in Italy to help put the country back together.

THE MARSHALL PLAN

In 1947, General George C. Marshall, the U.S. secretary of state, proposed a European Recovery Program, known as the Marshall Plan, to help revive the European economy after the devastation of World War II. The United States alone provided about $12 billion. Italy greatly benefited from the successful program.

Below: On June 4, 1944, Rome fell to the Allies, and U.S. jeeps from the Fifth Army entered Rome, cheered on by crowds of ecstatic Italians.

Relations between Italy and North America

Since World War II, much of the foreign relations between Italy and the United States has involved economic issues. The United States is one of Italy's most important trading partners.

Products such as office machinery, aircraft, industrial chemicals, and telecommunications equipment are principal U.S. exports to Italy. Other basic exports include frozen foods, bottled drinks, cereals, coal, and paper. Meanwhile, the United States imports Italian food, shoes, clothing, jewelry, marble, and ceramic tiles.

Formal government relations between Italy and the United States are warm and friendly. Italy occupies an important position in the Mediterranean, surrounded by unstable areas, such as the Balkans and the Middle East. So it benefits Italy and the United States to work together for peace and security, which they do through partnership in the United Nations and in the North Atlantic Treaty Organization (NATO), a defense treaty among the European nations and the United States. Italy also hosts U.S. military forces.

Above: **Former Italian prime minister Silvio Berlusconi and his wife met President and Mrs. Bill Clinton at the G-7 Summit held in Naples in 1994. On June 2 of the same year, the anniversary of Italy becoming a republic, President Clinton spoke in Rome. He said, "There is so much of Italy in America — art, music, philosophy, and, most important, the strength and wisdom of your sons and daughters. That bond of blood and spirit between our people is the heart and soul of our special relationship. America and Italy are more than mere partners, we are now…** *una famiglia* **(one family)."**

Italian-Americans

Many Italian immigrants who came to the United States spoke no English at first and had a difficult time finding a job. Many lived in poverty, and some were exploited in "sweatshops." Gradually, these immigrants adapted to their new country, learned the language, and began to improve their living conditions. One of the first to do this was a missionary nun, Mother Frances Cabrini, who was made a saint in 1946. She worked in the slums of Chicago, establishing schools, orphanages, and hospitals.

Another big success story was Amadeo Giannini. The son of Italian immigrants, he opened a small bank in San Francisco in 1904. By 1930, Giannini's bank, called the Bank of Italy, had changed its name to the Bank of America and become the largest in the United States! In politics, an influential Italian was Fiorello LaGuardia. He began his career as an interpreter at Ellis Island, studied law, then became a congressman and, in 1933, mayor of New York City. Arturo Toscanini, from Parma, Italy, became one of the most celebrated conductors in the United States.

Many Italian immigrants have been absorbed into the mainstream of American life. In fact, by the time the United States declared war on Italy in 1941, over 400,000 Italian-Americans were serving in the U.S. armed forces.

Americans in Italy

Italy has enchanted many American writers and artists. American painters, such as Benjamin West and Samuel F. B. Morse, lived in Italy to study the Old Masters. American writers, such as Nathaniel Hawthorne, Mark Twain, Edith Wharton, and Henry James, sought inspiration from the beauty and antiquity of the land. Twentieth century poet Ezra Pound chose to live in Italy. Harvard-educated art critic Bernard Berenson lived outside Florence until his death at the age of ninety-four. Writer Gore Vidal has made his home in Ravello, Italy.

Today, many Americans go to Italy to study. There are schools for language, art, archaeology, fashion design, cooking, tourism, gardening, photography, music, and even antique bookbinding. Some Italian-Americans also return to the towns of their birth, or to the towns of their ancestors, to retire. In addition, there are also about seventeen thousand American military personnel stationed at six different bases in Italy.

Top: **Academy Award winner, Al Pacino, has starred in many highly-acclaimed films.**

Center: **Director Martin Scorsese is an Italian-American renowned for his realistic, sometimes harsh, depictions of American culture in his films.**

Bottom: **The daughter of Italian immigrant parents, Geraldine Ferraro was the first woman nominated for vice presidency in the United States.**

Of Pasta, Pizza, and Wine

Italians did not deny their culture or lose their talents when they came to America. They shared them with their new friends.

What would American life be without Italian foods like pizza, spaghetti, *ravioli* (rah-vee-OH-lee), mozzarella, olive oil, Italian pastry, and wine!

In the United States, there are thousands of pizzerias, Italian restaurants in almost every city, bookstore racks lined with Italian cookbooks, supermarket shelves filled with packages of pasta, and television chefs teaching viewers to make homemade cannoli and other authentic Italian dishes. Italian foods have certainly crossed the Atlantic and become a permanent part of the American diet.

One of Italy's most important agricultural exports, olive oil, is also used increasingly in American dishes because it is known to be beneficial to health. As long as eight thousand years ago, olive oil was so valuable, it was traded for gold!

Below: **One of the most popular Italian foods in the United States is pizza. People like the fact that they can have all their favorite foods in one slice of pizza — just order one with "everything on it!"**

Made in Italy

Think of American life without gorgeous gowns by Armani, shiny shoes by Gucci, hand-tailored suits by Brioni, playclothes by Benetton, and black-rimmed glasses by Laura Biagiotti!

Maybe we cannot all afford these expensive Italian fashions, but we certainly see them on catwalks and on television. Hollywood stars dazzle us with their Italian gowns and jewelry at celebrity events. We also see Italian fashion in the movies. Tirelli, a costume house in Rome, furnished more than two hundred dresses for the movie *Titanic.*

Italy has made a great effort to sell fashions in the United States. The Italian Trade Commission has developed a program in Italy, called Moda Made, to educate the American consumer about the quality of Italian clothes, footwear, and accessories. Whether in Beverly Hills, Dallas, Chicago, Miami, or New York City, Americans can find "Made in Italy" labels.

The Internet has also become a popular shopping outlet for Italian clothes. Several websites have been developed where consumers can view and buy the latest designer fashions fresh from the catwalks of Milan.

Above: **Beverly Hills houses some of the most exclusive Italian fashion houses.**

	A	B	C	D

SWITZERLAND

Brenner Pass

AUSTRIA

HUNGARY

A

Monte Cervino
(14,780 ft /4,505 m)

Mont Blanc
(15,771 ft /
4807 m)

**VALLE
D'AOSTA**

Lake
Lugano

Lake
Orta

Lake
Maggiore

Lake
Como

Lake
Iseo

Lake
Garda

**TRENTINO-
ALTO
ADIGE**

Dolomites

**FRIULI-
VENEZIA
GIULIA**

SLOVENIA

CROATIA

1

FRANCE

Monza

Milan

Turin

LOMBARDY

PIEDMONT

Cremona

Po

Po *Valley*

A

p

e

Parma

EMILIA-ROMAGNA

Bologna

Castel San Pietro

VENETO

Verona

Padua

Po

Grado

Trieste

Venice

**BOSNIA
HERZEGOVINA**

LIGURIA

Genoa

MONACO

Carrara

Viareggio

Pisa

Arno

Florence

SAN MARINO

ADRIATIC

2

*LIGURIAN
SEA*

TUSCANY

Siena

Perugia

Fabriano

Nocera Umbra

Assisi

MARCHE

UMBRIA

Orvieto

SEA

Tiber

CORSICA

**VATICAN
CITY**

■ ROME

LATIUM

Nettuno

Anzio

ABRUZZI

MOLISE

Volturno

i

n

n

**APULIA
(PUGLIA)**

Bari

3

Mount Vesuvius
(4,190 ft/1,277 m) ▲

Pompeii

Ercolano (Resina)/

Naples

Torre Annunziata

Herculaneum

Capri

Ravello

Salerno

BASILICATA

SARDINIA

CAMPANIA

*TYRRHENIAN
SEA*

CALABRIA

N ▲

*IONIAN
SEA*

4

M E D I T E R R A N E A N

Stromboli

Vulcano

*Egadi
Islands*

Palermo

Messina

Mount Etna
(11,053 ft/3,369 m) ▲

Catania

S E A

SICILY

Agrigento

5

ALGERIA

TUNISIA

S E A

MALTA

—	State Boundary
■	Capital
●	City
～	River

ITALY

86

Above: Costumed revelers take time out for a pizza during the Carnival parade.

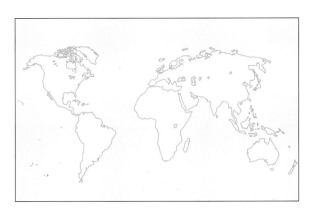

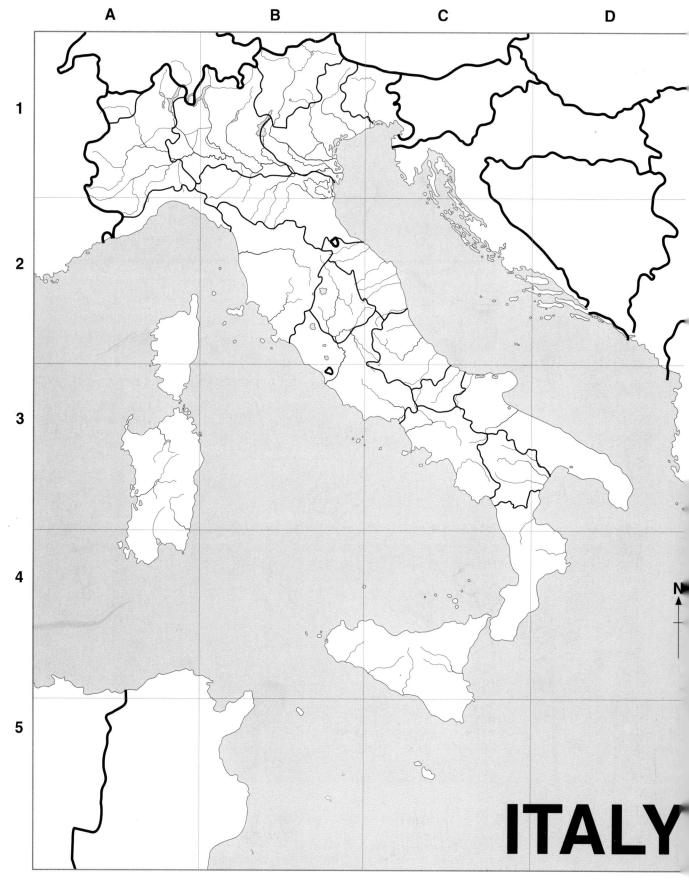

A B C D

1

2

3

4

5

N

ITALY

88

How Is Your Geography?

Learning to identify the main geographical areas and points of a country can be challenging. Although it may seem difficult at first to memorize the locations and spellings of major cities or the names of mountain ranges, rivers, deserts, lakes, and other prominent physical features, the end result of this effort can be very rewarding. Places you previously did not know existed will suddenly come to life when referred to in world news, whether in newspapers, television reports, or other books and reference sources. This knowledge will make you feel a bit closer to the rest of the world, with its fascinating variety of cultures and physical geography.

Used in a classroom setting, the instructor can make duplicates of this map using a copy machine. (PLEASE DO NOT WRITE IN THIS BOOK!) Students can then fill in any requested information on their individual map copies. Used one-on-one, the student can also make copies of the map on a copy machine and use them as a study tool. The student can practice identifying place names and geographical features on his or her own.

Above: **A store sells spices to flavor Italian foods.**

Italy at a Glance

Official Name	Republic of Italy (Repubblica Italiana)
Capital	Rome
Official Language	Italian
Population	58,138,000
Land Area	116,333 square miles (301,302 square km)
Regions	Abruzzi, Apulia (Puglia), Basilicata, Calabria, Campania, Emilia-Romagna, Friuli-Venezia Giulia, Latium, Liguria, Lombardy, Marche, Molise, Piedmont, Sardinia, Sicily, Trentino-Alto Adige, Tuscany, Umbria, Valle d'Aosta, Veneto
Highest Point	Mont Blanc (15,771 feet/4,807 m)
Longest River	Po River (416 miles/670 km)
Major Cities	Rome, Milan, Naples, Turin, Genoa, Palermo, Bologna, Florence, Catania, Bari, Venice
Borders	France, Switzerland, Austria, and Slovenia
Coastline	5,310 miles (8, 544 km)
Climate	Alpine in the north, hot and dry in the south
Major Mountains	Alps, Dolomites (part of the Alpine range), and Apennines; volcanoes include Mount Etna and Mount Vesuvius
Major Lakes	Como, Garda, Iseo, Lugano, Maggiore, Orta
Islands	Sicily, Sardinia, Elba, Capri, Ischia, the Aeolian Islands, the Egadi Islands, Pantelleria, Ustica, Asinara, La Maddalena, Caprera, Tremiti
Major Religion	Roman Catholicism (95 percent)
Currency	Italian lira (1,665 lire = U.S. $1 as of 1999)

Opposite: **Construction of the Leaning Tower of Pisa was started in 1174. When three of its eight stories were completed, it started leaning, due to uneven settling of its foundation in the soft ground.**

Glossary

Italian Vocabulary

antipasti (ahn-tee-PAHS-tee): appetizers.

bella figura (BEH-la fee-GOO-rah): style.

bianco (bee-AHN-koh): white (official Italian).

cannelloni (kah-neh-LOH-nee): pasta shaped into tubular casings filled with meat and sauce.

cannoli (kah-NOH-lee): Italian pastry formed in tubes, deep fried, and filled with cheese and other ingredients.

cappuccino (kah-pooh-CHEE-noh): coffee with steamed milk.

Chianti (kee-AHN-tee): popular Italian red wine from the Tuscany region.

contrada (cone-TRAH-dah): neighborhood or regional group.

espresso (ehs-PREH-soh): a type of concentrated coffee.

gelato (jeh-LAH-toh): ice cream.

harpastum (HAHR-pah-stoom): game played by ancient Romans, in which two teams try to push a ball over lines drawn behind the opponents.

liceo (lee-CHAY-oh): academic school.

mafiosi (mah-fee-OH-zee): members of organized crime.

magistrale (mah-gee-STRAH-lay): a school for teachers.

minestrone (mee-neh-STROH-nay): thick vegetable soup.

palio (PAH-lee-oh): banner.

passeggiata (pah-seh-jee-AH-tah): a walk or stroll.

pastina (pahs-TEE-nah): small forms of pasta for children.

pesto (PEH-stoh): a sauce made from olive oil, spices, and pine nuts.

piazza (pee-AH-tsah): an open place in a city.

prosciutto (proh-SHOO-toh): spicy Italian ham.

regionalismo (REE-gee-oh-nah-LEEZ-moh): regional loyalty.

Risorgimento (ree-sor-gee-MEN-toh): a movement for Italian reunification in the nineteenth century.

risotto (ree-SOH-toh): rice.

sala da pranzo (SAH-lah dah PRAHN-zoh): small dining room.

salotto (sah-LOH-toh): living room.

solo (SOH-loh): alone.

tifosi (tee-FOH-see): (soccer) fans.

tortellini (tohr-teh-LEE-nee): stuffed pasta.

vaporettos (vah-poh-RET-tohs): boats powered by motors.

vermicelli (vehr-mee-CHEH-lee): pasta shaped like little worms.

zuppa inglese (ZUH-pah een-gleh-ZEE): cake drenched in rum with custard and whipped cream.

English Vocabulary

alliance: an association formed to work toward a common goal.

anesthetized: to be unconscious or unable to feel pain after being given a drug, especially during operations and surgical procedures.

aristocrats: people from families of high social status. Many aristocrats are nobles, with special titles.

authoritarian: related to a government or leader that enforces unquestioning obedience to authority.

bewitched: to be charmed, enchanted, or fascinated by something or someone.

billowing: rising slowly upward with a wavelike swelling or rolling motion.

boisterous: noisy and lively.

compulsory: mandatory; must be done.

coveted: desired.

culinary: related to cooking.

dictator: a ruler with absolute power and authority.

dissent: disagreement or protest.

electorate: all the people in a region who have the right to vote in an election.

elusive: difficult to achieve.

evacuate: to move away from a place because it poses some danger.

fascism: a set of political beliefs that includes control of society and economy by the state, total suppression of opposition, and increased power of the armed forces.

flamboyant: extravagant or showy.

frescoes: pictures painted on plastered walls when the plaster is still wet.

gnarled: twisted and oddly shaped, often because of old age.

heritage: culture and traditions passed down from our ancestors.

incentives: things that encourage a person or group to take action.

indulge: to do something for enjoyment.

lavish: abundant and extravagant.

medieval: related to the Middle Ages, or the period in European history between A.D. 476 and 1450.

ornate: heavily ornamented, or decorated.

peninsula: a land area surrounded on three sides by water and connected to the mainland on one side.

persecution: cruel and unfair treatment of an individual or group usually due to religion, race, or political beliefs.

poignantly: in an emotionally touching or moving way.

precision: accuracy.

principal: first in order of importance.

regionalism: the pride that people of a particular region have for that region, which usually develops its own customs, language, etc.

resplendent: impressive and splendid in appearance.

revolutionized: changed drastically.

scabbards: sheaths, or cases, for swords.

seismic: related to earthquakes.

sinister: evil, wicked, or dishonest; threatening harm.

spewed: ejected violently in large quantities.

strenuous: requiring a large amount of effort and energy.

suburbs: residential areas on the outskirts of a town or city.

susceptible: having a high likelihood of being influenced by something.

unrivaled: better than others of its kind; having no rivals, competitors, or equals.

venerated: worshiped or revered; showed or felt great respect for someone or something.

vernacular: the everyday language spoken by ordinary people in a country or region.

vocational: related to education and training that teaches skills needed for a particular profession or occupation.

More Books to Read

The History of Emigration from Italy. Origins series. Katherine Prior and Katherine Powell (Franklin Watts)

Italian Americans. Cultures of America series. Carolyn Washburne (Marshall Cavendish Corporation)

Italian Renaissance. Living History series. John D. Clare, ed. (Gulliver Books)

Italy. Country Fact Files series. Derek Allen (Raintree Steck-Vaughn)

Italy. Festivals of the World series. Elizabeth Berg (Gareth Stevens)

Italy and Italian. Getting to Know series. Emma Sansone (Barrons Juveniles)

Leonardo da Vinci: Artist, Inventor, and Scientist of the Renaissance. Francesca Romei (Peter Bedrick Books)

Pompeii: The Day a City Was Buried. DK Discoveries series. Christopher Rice and Melanie Rice (DK Publishing)

Rome. Cities of the World series. Richard Conrad Stein (Childrens Press)

A Taste of Italy. Food Around the World series. Jenny Ridgwell (Thomson Learning)

Videos

Discovering Italy. (International Video Network)

Rome. (International Video Network)

Touring Italy. (Questar Video)

Web Sites

www.city.net/countries/italy/

www.arcaini.com/Italy%20history.html

www.Italyemb.org/

www.wonderful-italy.it/main.html

Due to the dynamic nature of the Internet, some web sites stay current longer than others. To find additional web sites, use reliable search engines with one or more of the following keywords to help you locate information on Italy. Keywords: *Italy, Julius Caesar, pasta, pizza, pope, Renaissance, Rome, Venice.*

Index